CHRISTIAN HEROES: THEN & NOW

GLADYS AYLWARD

The Adventure of a Lifetime

CHRISTIAN HEROES: THEN & NOW

GLADYS AYLWARD

The Adventure of a Lifetime

JANET & GEOFF BENGE

YWAM
PUBLISHING
P.O. BOX 55787   SEATTLE, WA 98155

YWAM Publishing is the publishing ministry of Youth With A Mission. Youth With A Mission (YWAM) is an international missionary organization of Christians from many denominations dedicated to presenting Jesus Christ to this generation. To this end, YWAM has focused its efforts in three main areas: (1) training and equipping believers for their part in fulfilling the Great Commission (Matthew 28:19), (2) personal evangelism, and (3) mercy ministry (medical and relief work).

For a free catalog of books and materials, contact:

YWAM Publishing
P.O. Box 55787, Seattle, WA 98155
(425) 771-1153 or (800) 922-2143
www.ywampublishing.com

Library of Congress Cataloging-in-Publication Data

Benge, Janet, 1958–
    Gladys Aylward : the adventure of a lifetime / Janet and Geoff Benge.
        p. cm. — (Christian heroes, then & now)
    Includes bibliographical references.
    Summary: Recounts the life story of the Englishwoman who financed her own overland trip to China to become a missionary.
    ISBN 1-57658-019-9
    1. Aylward, Gladys—Juvenile literature. 2. Missionaries—China—Biography—Juvenile literature. 3. Missionaries—English—Biography—Juvenile literature. [1. Aylward, Gladys.
    2. Missionaries. 3. Women—Biography.] I. Benge, Geoff, 1954–
    II. Title. III. Series.
    BV3427.A9B46 1998
    266'.0092—dc21
    [B]   98-19368
                                                              CIP
                                                              AC

Gladys Aylward: The Adventure of a Lifetime
Copyright © 1998 by YWAM Publishing

10 09 08 07 06   10

Published by Youth With A Mission Publishing
P.O. Box 55787
Seattle, WA 98155

ISBN 1-57658-019-9

Printed in the United States of America.

CHRISTIAN HEROES: THEN & NOW
Biographies

*Unit study curriculum guides are
available for select biographies.*

Available at your local Christian bookstore or
from YWAM Publishing • 1-800-922-2143

Special thanks to our daughter Shannon for her help in preparing this manuscript.

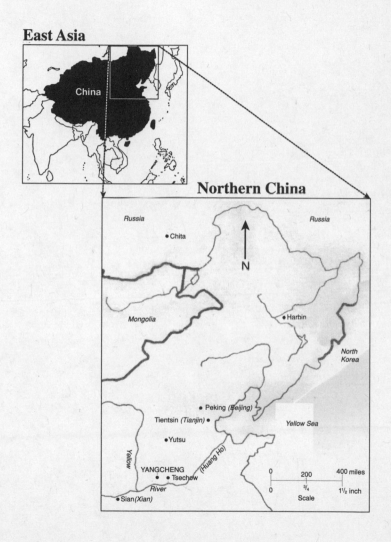

East Asia

China

Northern China

Russia

• Chita

N

Russia

Mongolia

• Harbin

North
Korea

Peking (Beijing) •

Tientsin (Tianjin) •

Yellow Sea

• Yutsu

Yellow

YANGCHENG
• • Tsechow

River

(Huang Ho)

• Sian (Xian)

| 0 | | 200 | | 400 miles |
| 0 | | ³/₄ | | 1¹/₂ inch |

Scale

Contents

Chapter 1

Back up the Tracks

Gladys Aylward pulled herself up to her full five-foot height as she peered over the edge of the wooden train platform. Eerie flashes of orange light lit up the sky and the forest to the east. Loud cracks of gunfire and the boom of cannons rolled through the darkness. Ahead lay the railroad tracks. Even though the train had rumbled down them less than an hour ago, they were already covered with the powdery snow that continued to fall, blanketing everything.

Gladys pulled her fur coat tight around her and shuddered. She didn't want to step off the platform and begin her trek, but she had no choice. The only reason she had no choice now was that she had refused to get off the train earlier when asked to, and the frustrated conductor had allowed her to stay on board as the train wound its way through the Siberian forest. Now Gladys chided herself for being so stubborn and not getting off the train in Chita, as everyone else had. But she'd thought that every mile traveled down the line was a mile closer to China. And it was. But it was also a mile traveled farther into a war zone!

It had all looked so easy back at Muller's Shipping Agency in Haymarket, London, where the clerk had traced out the route on a map. "Over the English Channel by boat from Hull," he had said. "Board the train in The Hague, Holland, and overland through Germany, Poland, Russia, Siberia, and on to Tientsin in China."

Gladys frowned. As easy as he had made it sound at the time, the clerk had also mentioned that there was a war going on in Siberia. But to Gladys, then twenty-eight years old, it seemed an unimportant detail in the grand scheme of getting herself to China. Now she found herself in the middle of that unimportant detail! The train she'd been riding was stopped at the front line of the little war going on between Russia and China. It had delivered fresh Russian soldiers and now waited to pick up the dead and wounded and carry them away from the front. But how long it would take to fill up the train with the dead and wounded was anyone's guess. Perhaps a week. Perhaps a month. Possibly not until the New Year, 1931! No one seemed to know.

Finally, the frustrated conductor had given Gladys a cup of strong, black coffee and pointed back up the railroad tracks in the direction from which they had come. Although he spoke no English, his message was clear: Gladys was not welcome to stay and wait for the return train ride. She was going to have to walk back to Chita.

With her bags in hand, Gladys finally stepped down onto the railroad tracks and began her trek. As she walked, she recalled the landscape. She hadn't seen a single person, not even the light from a house or a barn, on the journey down. For thirty miles there was nothing but thick, dark forest.

An icy wind whipped at Gladys's exposed face. Gladys could feel its bitter cold seep through her woolen stockings and sweater. With each whip of the wind around her, she felt her strength being sapped. Soon she could no longer carry her bags, so she slid them along on the snow. Her smaller bag had a pot and a kettle tied to its outside that jangled loudly with each slide.

Gladys had been stumbling along for about an hour when she realized that the orange glow of cannon fire was no longer on the horizon. Even though she'd been at the front line, the thought of people being nearby had been strangely comforting. Now she was completely alone in the vast Siberian wilderness, trudging along snow-covered train tracks. Every so often, a large clump of snow slipped off a tree limb and landed with a loud thud. Gladys would stop and peer into the dark shadows of the forest and wonder whether it was the sound of a bear or a wolf nearby. Such animals were out there, and a lone woman in the forest at night was easy prey for them.

Gladys began wondering whether she would actually make it back to Chita, or whether the bitter cold or a wild beast would claim her life first. But she had to make it back. She had things to do in China. God had called her there. Surely He wouldn't let her die in the snow in a Siberian forest.

Slowly Gladys shuffled on up the tracks. The hours folded one into another. Her feet became numb, and she began dragging and sliding them along just as she did her two suitcases. But stubborn as she was, Gladys finally had to admit she was totally exhausted. What should she do? If she stopped she could make herself some hot coffee and eat a stale cookie. But would she be able to go on after that? She'd heard stories of people who when trapped in the cold and snow had become so exhausted they calmly sat down and froze to death. Gladys was scared of that happening to her. Yet she knew that if she kept going, in the end she would fall facedown in the snow. Then, with nothing warm in her stomach, she would not have the energy to get up again.

Finally, she could no longer resist the lure of a stale cookie and hot cup of coffee. She scooped away the snow until she felt one of the wooden railroad ties beneath it. With both hands she took her small spirit stove from her bag, set it down on the tie, and tried to light it. Her fingers where so thick and numb that it took her four fumbled attempts before a yellow-blue flame finally began to glow from the stove. Gladys placed some snow into the kettle and set the kettle on the stove to melt and boil the snow.

With a cookie and hot coffee inside her, Gladys felt even more tired. But she dared not sleep in this frozen wasteland. In the end, though, she gave in, but she promised herself that she would sleep for only a little while. She arranged her suitcases around herself and pulled the top of her fur coat up over her head. Then she rolled up into a ball and fell asleep.

Chapter 2

Not Good Enough to Be a Missionary

Her worst nightmare had come true. Gladys sat in a straight-backed chair while the director of the China Inland Missionary Society's training school in London droned on. By now she was hardly listening to what he had to say. All that needed to be said had already been said. Gladys was no longer welcome to continue her studies. She was being thrown out of the training school for failing Bible class. Her grades were not good enough for her to be a missionary. Not to mention the fact that she was twenty-seven years of age, old by the training school's standards. The director had tried to explain that the experience of the China Inland Mission had shown that it was difficult enough for "quick-minded" older people to learn the complex languages of China. He also tried to explain that it would be unfair to allow Gladys to continue failing classes when others could take her place and do much better. Other younger and more-qualified people were waiting in line to take her place in the school.

The director was a kindly man with deep blue eyes and a soft voice. He wasn't trying to hurt Gladys's feelings. He was just giving her the facts as they were. Gladys could see his point. She hadn't done well during the first three months of the school. But then she'd never done well at school. She had left school at age fourteen to take a job as a housemaid. And by missionary standards, she was an older woman, though she didn't feel it. If she stayed in the training school to the end, she would be thirty years old by the time she got to China. At that age it would probably be difficult for her to learn Chinese. It was also true she had no useful qualifications. She wasn't a nurse or a teacher. She was just Gladys Aylward, daughter of Thomas and Rosina Aylward, a postman and a housewife from Edmonton, a small suburb of London.

Even though she understood all this, tears of disappointment welled in Gladys's eyes as the young woman stood to leave the director's office. Gladys didn't trust herself to speak without bursting into loud sobs. Instead, she thrust out her hand to shake the director's hand. He was about to shake her hand when he hesitated. "One more thing, Miss

Aylward," he said. "There is one way you could serve God with regard to China."

Gladys's heart skipped a beat. Was she going to get to China some other way, after all?

The director continued. "I see you've been in service before as a housemaid."

"Yes," replied Gladys, wondering what was coming next.

"As it happens," the director went on, "I received news this morning of an elderly missionary couple, Dr. and Mrs. Fisher, who have just returned from China. They have retired to Bristol and need a housemaid. I would be more than happy to recommend you for the job."

Gladys clutched the back of the chair. Her head was spinning. After all her effort to make her dream of going to China as a missionary come to pass, the director thought she was fit only to be a housemaid. Her shoulders slumped as she sat down again to copy the Fishers' address.

Dr. and Mrs. Fisher turned out to be not at all like Gladys had imagined them. They didn't need much help around the house, and they were still very interested in missionary work. They listened to Gladys's story of how she had grown up in a Christian home, though Christianity hadn't come alive to her until one night two years before when she had visited an unfamiliar church. She had heard a young preacher tell about the many wonderful missionary opportunities that existed, especially in

China. Something inside Gladys was stirred that night, and she knew she wanted to serve God as a missionary in China.

Gladys asked the Fishers all sorts of questions about China and wrote their answers in her journal.

Because the Fishers were so kind, Gladys didn't mind being their housemaid. Dr. and Mrs. Fisher became concerned for Gladys, however. They could see that Gladys had too much enthusiasm and energy to limit herself to being a housemaid. They didn't see how she would ever get to China, but they did think she should find some full-time Christian work where her talents could be put to better use. They knew the director of a rescue mission in Swansea, a seaport in south Wales. They contacted him, and he invited Gladys to work for the mission as a "rescue sister." The job involved patrolling the streets of Swansea in the middle of the night looking for young girls who had no place to stay. Many of the girls had come to the city to escape the boredom of their villages but quickly ran out of money after they arrived. With no money for food or rent, they began living on the streets. Often, out of desperation, they became involved in prostitution as a way to make ends meet. A rescue sister's job was to find these girls before the sailors did. The mission would pay for the girls to stay one night in a hostel and in the morning would put them on a train back home to their villages.

Gladys's parents had never tried to shelter their daughter from the way other people lived. Even so,

Gladys was shocked at the way these girls lived on the street each night. Yet Gladys loved the job. She especially liked it when she got to share the gospel message with the girls. As much as she loved the job, though, something was missing. Yes, she was doing very useful work, but she wasn't doing it in China, where she knew God wanted her to be.

Gladys knew, of course, that after her mission training school experience no missionary organization would send her to China. If she was going to go there, she would have to get there on her own. But she had no money, and her parents were not rich. Nor did she have any rich friends who would sponsor her. She had only one option: She would have to save up the money to pay her own way to China. Much as she loved being a rescue sister, she needed a job that paid more money. The little she did get paid by the rescue mission usually ended up buying food for the girls who were going home. The job she knew best, and the job where she knew she could earn enough money to save some, was being a housemaid again. With a heavy heart at leaving the job in Swansea she enjoyed so much, she returned to London to find work as a housemaid.

In London, the employment agency sent her to work at the home of Sir Francis Younghusband. Gladys pulled the silver bell at the door of the huge house in Belgravia, near Buckingham Palace. A butler answered the door and showed Gladys to her new room. The room had a bed, a chair, and a water stand, like most maid's rooms. Gladys lifted her cardboard suitcase onto the bed. Inside it was everything she owned. She pulled out her black leather-bound Bible and placed it carefully on the chair beside her bed. Next she reached into her purse and took out all the money she had left after getting to Belgravia. She didn't need to count it; she knew exactly how much she had. After paying the train fare from Edmonton, where she had visited her parents, Gladys had two and a half pennies left. She laid them in a row on top of her Bible. A sense of hopelessness came over her. What was the use of trying to save enough money to get to China when traveling across London had taken nearly all the money she had?

Then Gladys thought about why she wanted to go to China. She was certain it was where God wanted her to live and work, and if that was where He wanted her, surely He would help her get the money she needed to get there. She placed her hands over the money and in a loud voice prayed, "Here is my Bible. Here is all the money I have. Here is me. Find some way to use me, God!"

As she prayed, the door creaked open, and another maid peered into her room. Gladys knew that the maid must have heard her prayer, but she didn't care; she had meant every word she prayed.

"Excuse me," began the maid, "but the mistress wants to see you in the drawing room."

Gladys glanced in the mirror and quickly adjusted her black bun. She stepped into the hallway and followed the maid down the servants' stairs to the drawing room, where Lady Annabel Younghusband was waiting for her. Gladys curtsied and introduced herself.

Lady Annabel smiled at her. "How much did the train fare to get here cost you?" she asked Gladys kindly.

"Two shillings and nine pence, ma'am," Gladys replied, wondering why the woman was asking such a question.

"Here you are," Lady Annabel said, reaching into her purse. "Take three shillings. I always pay the fare of my maids when I hire them."

Gladys could hardly believe it. No one had ever before offered to pay her train fare to get to a new job. She thanked Lady Annabel and bounded back up the stairs to her room. She put the three shillings next to the two and a half pennies. A big smile lit up her face. In the ten minutes since praying her prayer, her money had increased fifteen times! In her mind, Gladys was already practically in China!

Of course, Gladys had no idea how much a trip to China would cost. It wasn't the kind of thing her parents or any of the other maids knew, either. But she needed to find out. So as she polished the silverware and dusted books over the next several days, Gladys worked out a plan. She would save every penny she could, and when she had saved three pounds, she would go to Haymarket and find a shipping agent. There she would put a deposit on a ticket to China.

It didn't take Gladys as long as she thought to save three pounds. She managed to find some extra work serving at banquets in the evenings and on her days off. Several weeks later, with high hopes, she caught a trolley car to Haymarket. The trolley stopped right outside the door to Muller's Shipping Agency.

Gathering all her courage, Gladys pushed open the door to Muller's and entered the impressive building. It was just about empty inside, so she did not have to wait long before being served. She cleared her throat and looked directly at the elderly clerk who had asked if he could help her. "How much is a one-way ticket to China?" she politely asked.

"And to what part of China would that be?" the clerk snapped back.

Gladys hadn't thought about that. "I don't know," she stammered, feeling her cheeks turning red with embarrassment at the question. "Any part will do. Whatever is the cheapest to get to."

The clerk looked at her patched coat and threadbare gloves and rolled his eyes as if to say he didn't have time for a maid pretending to be rich. Gladys obviously looked like a person who would never be able to afford a trip to China. "Please step aside, Miss. I have work to do," he finally said in a firm voice.

"No, you don't understand," Gladys pleaded. "I have money, and I need to get to China." She fumbled in her pocket and pulled out the three one-pound notes. "Here," she continued, laying the notes on the counter between them.

The clerk sighed. "Ma'am, the cheapest sea passage to any part of China," he explained, emphasizing the word *any*, "is ninety pounds. That's thirty times more than the money you have."

Gladys felt sick. Ninety pounds would take forever to save. She knew the clerk expected her to pick up the money and walk out, but she did not. "There must be a cheaper way," she asked, trying to sound calm.

The clerk sighed heavily again. "There is, ma'am," he said, unable to keep the sarcasm from his voice, "if you don't mind arriving dead, that is."

Gladys stared at him and waited for him to continue.

"There is a rail route through Europe, Russia, and Siberia to Tientsin in northern China. It would cost forty-seven pounds ten shillings. But a war is in progress between Russia and China over a land claim in the area. It's unlikely you would arrive alive at your destination, wherever that might be."

Gladys leveled her dark brown eyes at the clerk and spoke calmly. "It's my life that would be at risk, so it's my choice. Do you or do you not sell train tickets to China?"

The clerk nodded. "Yes, we do," he said.

"Very well," said Gladys. "I would like to open an account to pay for a train ticket to China. Take the three pounds, and I'll be back every Friday afternoon with more money until I have paid the ticket off." Then, feeling she might have been a little overly bold, Gladys added with a smile, "Don't worry about me and a silly little war. By the time I save enough money to get to China, it will be long over."

Seeing that Gladys was not going to leave until he took her money, the clerk counted her three one-pound notes into the money drawer and wrote her a receipt. Then, reluctantly, he opened the company ledger and asked Gladys for her name and address.

Gladys left Muller's Shipping Agency a very happy person. She had just paid three pounds deposit on a ticket to China. She only had forty-four pounds ten shillings to go.

As she rode the trolley back to Belgravia, she turned her attention to what she would do once she got to China. She needed more training, but where would she get it? She didn't want to spend any money on Bible school. Besides, she'd already failed at that! If she was going to get an education in missionary work, Gladys decided she was going to have to give it to herself.

On a piece of paper she noted some of the things she'd need to learn. The first thing on her list was preaching. Every missionary needed to know how to preach, she told herself. Hyde Park in London became the place where she learned to do this. Hyde Park was where people with strong opinions climbed onto wooden soapboxes and made speeches. Most of the speeches were about politics. If a passerby liked what the person was saying, he or she might stop and listen for a while, perhaps even throw a penny or two at the speaker's feet. Those who disagreed might jeer and throw a leftover sandwich from lunch at the speaker. In the midst of the loud, bustling crowd, Gladys, wearing a simple black dress, would climb onto her soapbox and begin preaching at the top of her voice. She preached about how much God loved the people hurrying by and about their need to serve God.

Nobody stopped to listen to her. A few people passing by jeered and heckled her, but Gladys did not mind. Each time she got up to preach, she was a little less concerned about what people thought of her and a little more confident that one day she would preach in China.

Besides learning to preach, Gladys set out to learn more about China. This task was made easier for her by a happy coincidence. Sir Francis Younghusband was a famous explorer who had spent a lot of time in the interior of China and had written several books on his experiences there. Gladys politely asked him if she could borrow some of the books from his private library. He was puzzled. Housemaids were usually not interested much in reading, especially not the type of books he had in his library. Though the request seemed odd, Sir Francis Younghusband kindly told Gladys she could borrow one book at a time from his library and keep it for a week.

As with her preaching in Hyde Park, Gladys threw herself into reading as many books about

China from her employer's library as she possibly could. As she read each book, she made notes about what she'd learned in the journal she'd started while working for the Fishers.

Things for her trip to China were slowly coming together. But Gladys still had a few unanswered questions. Where would she go, and what would she do once she got there?

Chapter 3

All Aboard

Gladys hadn't really been paying much attention to the elderly woman talking to her after church. She was tired from the late party she had been serving at the night before. But as exhausted as she felt, the extra work was worth it to her. In only seven months she had deposited nearly all the money for her ticket to China at Muller's Shipping Agency. Every week the clerk, who now looked forward to her visits to pay more money on the ticket, would ask her whether she knew yet where she was going in China. And each week Gladys told him she didn't. But as she stood, tired, not really paying too much attention to the old woman, her ears suddenly pricked up.

"As I was saying," the old lady said, "Mrs. Lawson couldn't settle back into England after her husband died. Last year she packed up everything and went back to China. She said she would rather die there doing God's work than stay in England doing needlepoint. At seventy-three years old, I expect she will die there."

"Did you say she's gone back to China?" asked Gladys.

"Yes," said the woman. "Her only regret was that she had to go back alone. She couldn't interest anyone in going back with her. It's a pity, really; she wanted to train someone to carry on after she was gone."

Gladys could feel the hairs on the back of her neck stand on end. "That's me," she blurted, before she even knew what she was saying.

The old woman looked at Gladys in amazement. But over the next several minutes, Gladys managed to convinced her she was serious about going to China. So the woman searched around in her huge handbag until she found Mrs. Lawson's address. She handed it to Gladys, kissed her on the cheek, and wished her well.

Gladys went back to her room at the Younghusbands' house in Belgravia full of enthusiasm. She had so many things to do. She had to write to Mrs. Lawson and let her know help was on the way, and she had to tell the clerk at Muller's Shipping Agency she now had a destination in China. She also had to collect as many useful items as she could for her trip to China.

It wasn't too long before Gladys received a letter from Mrs. Lawson telling her that if she came to China she had work for her, and she would meet Gladys in Tientsin. So, on Saturday, October 15, 1930, three months after hearing about Mrs. Lawson, Gladys stood at the Liverpool Street railway station, ready to begin her journey. She was by far the strangest-looking passenger waiting to board the train, wearing a bright orange dress and a huge fur overcoat with the sleeves cut out. The coat was far too heavy for the English autumn she was leaving behind. Under her clothes she was wearing one of her mother's old corsets. Sewn inside the corset was a maze of secret pockets holding her train tickets, passport, a fountain pen (which she hoped wouldn't leak), all her money (nine pennies in loose change and two one-pound traveler's checks), and her Bible. Of course, these items stuffed inside her corset made her look rather lumpy, but fortunately, the fur overcoat managed to hide most of the lumps.

Gladys also had with her two old, battered suitcases. In the larger of the two suitcases she had packed some extra clothes: darned woolen stockings, a hand-knitted sweater from her sister Violet, and a woolly vest from a woman at church. A bedroll and a small spirit stove were also packed inside. The smaller suitcase was filled with food: canned fish and meat, baked beans, crackers, boiled eggs, instant coffee, and lots of tea. On its outside was tied a large pot and a kettle. Altogether, Gladys looked more like a hobo than a departing missionary.

"All aboard for Hull," yelled the conductor. Steam hissed from the huge locomotive at the front of the train. Gladys hugged her parents and Violet good-bye. Her brother Lawrence, a drummer in the British Army, wasn't able to be there, but Gladys had a photo of him in his full-dress uniform tucked into her suitcase.

"Don't forget us, Glad," said Violet, as she gave her big sister one last hug.

"Our Glad will never forget us, will you, love?" said her mother. "And we'll be praying for you every day," she added, giving Gladys a motherly pat on the hand.

Gladys surveyed the crowd of about fifty people who'd come to wish her well. Even the clerk from Muller's Shipping Agency was there. Gladys tried to take in every detail so she would always remember the people who had loved and supported her as she worked to make her dream of going to China come true.

Another loud hiss of steam escaped from the locomotive, and Gladys climbed into the carriage. She pulled down the window and waved furiously to everyone. The conductor blew his whistle, and the train began to pull away from the platform. Slowly, Gladys's friends, relatives, and supporters grew smaller and smaller in the distance, until

Gladys sat alone on the train. She was bound for Tientsin, China, with two pounds nine shillings tucked in a pocket in her corset.

It didn't take Gladys long to make friends on the train. A middle-aged couple took a special interest in her. They had seen all the people farewelling her in London and asked where she was going. Gladys told them that she was on her way to be a missionary in China. The train she was on would take her to Hull, where she would catch a boat to The Hague in Holland. There she would board another train and travel overland through Germany, Poland, and Russia to China.

The couple turned out to be Christians and were on their way back to Holland after attending some Keswick meetings in England. As the English countryside rolled by, Gladys and the couple became firm friends. The three of them boarded the boat for The Hague together, and as the Dutch coastline came into view, the couple made Gladys a promise. They would pray for her every night at 9 P.M. for the rest of their lives. As the couple said good-bye to Gladys on the train in The Hague, the husband shook Gladys's hand heartily, and his wife kissed Gladys good-bye, as if she were her own sister.

It was not until Gladys had settled into her seat and the train had pulled away from the station that she noticed that the husband had pressed something into her hand. She turned her hand over, and when she opened it, in her palm was a crumpled one-pound note. Gladys was very grateful for the money, though she didn't know what use English money would be where she was going. But it was kind of him. As soon as she could, she folded the one-pound note, tucked it into one of the pockets in her corset, and quickly forgot about it.

Cities and villages, barns and bridges flashed by as the train wound its way across Europe. Slowly the plains turned into rolling hills, and then the hills turned into mountains. All the while, Gladys sat with her nose up against the carriage window, fascinated by all she was seeing. The farther away the train got from The Hague, the fewer the fellow passengers who spoke English. In Berlin, Germany, Gladys had a difficult time making herself understood to the immigration officer, but thankfully he recognized her British passport and waved her through. The train continued on through Warsaw, Moscow, Irkutsk, and on past Lake Baikal.

Gladys ate meals she made from the food in her suitcase. The eggs her mother had boiled for her she ate in Warsaw, the canned herring in Moscow, and the crackers and cheese while watching Lake Baikal glide by. The only exercise Gladys got on the trip was walking up and down the carriage aisle or walking briskly around the train when it stopped to take on more coal and water for the engine.

Seven days after leaving the Liverpool Street station, Gladys crossed the Ural Mountains that divide Europe from Asia. The first difference she noticed as the train moved across eastern Russia was the extreme cold. Each carriage had small steam radiators for heat, but even sitting sideways with her back against a radiator provided Gladys little heat against the freezing wind that whipped into the train around the edges of the windows. So Gladys kept her fur coat pulled tightly around her.

The next difference that Gladys noted in this part of Russia was the type of passengers on the train. At each stop, more grandmothers and businessmen got off the train, and more soldiers climbed on. By the time the train crossed into Siberia, Gladys was the only civilian on board. This made her very nervous at first. The Russian soldiers were loud and unshaven. Under their arms they carried long loaves of bread, from which they broke off and ate chunks when they were hungry. Any English girl would have found their manners revolting. They ate with their mouths wide open and blew their noses into their fingers. It was hard for Gladys to keep smiling at them. She tried to think of her brother Lawrence. She took his photo from her bag and studied it carefully. He looked handsome in his full-dress uniform. Gladys reminded herself that the soldier sitting next to her, laughing and slapping his friend on the shoulder, was probably someone's brother. Gladys was grateful that these loud and a bit unruly soldiers were at least polite to her.

After passing Lake Baikal, the train headed southwest in the direction of Harbin, China, where Gladys would transfer to a Manchurian railway train to continue her journey to Tientsin. As darkness fell, the train rumbled on. Gladys dropped off to sleep with her shoulder leaning against the icy window of the carriage.

Gladys awoke sometime later to the conductor yelling at her. She couldn't understand a word he was saying, of course, but she got the general idea from his actions. He pointed to the small station where the train had stopped, and then he pointed at Gladys and her baggage. He wanted Gladys to take her luggage and get off the train. Gladys shook her head and pulled her two suitcases down from the overhead rack. She stacked them on the floor and sat on them. She decided her little demonstration would get the message across to the conductor that she wouldn't be getting off the train. The conductor continued yelling at her for several minutes, but Gladys just pulled out her ticket and pointed to the destination of Tientsin, China, written on it. He threw up his hands in disbelief. One last time the conductor tried to convince her to get off. He pretended to shoot a gun and then clutched his chest as if wounded. Still Gladys wouldn't budge. She had a ticket to China, and every turn of the train wheels down the tracks was a wheel turn closer to her destination. Eventually, the conductor gave up in disgust, and a short while later the train lurched away from the Chita railway station.

The train moved through the black Siberian night. Trees lined the railroad tracks and towered menacingly above the train. Gladys was glad to be tucked in her warm coat inside the train with its lights and heaters. She was even glad for her noisy fellow travelers. The train was now completely filled with soldiers, but their presence gave Gladys courage as they passed through the lonely, desolate countryside. It was very late in the evening when the train whistle sounded and the engine hissed to a stop. A Russian officer stood and yelled something at the men. The soldiers grabbed their knapsacks and formed a line outside the carriage. Gladys watched them march on down the tracks, their breath forming white puffs in the icy darkness. In the distance, wolves howled.

Gladys turned away from the window just as the train was plunged into blackness. She waited for her eyes to adjust to the dark. She listened carefully; the train was no longer hissing. A thought occurred to her that caused her to panic. What if the train had stopped here for good? She grabbed her suitcases and made her way down the aisle to the end of the carriage. Suddenly an unfamiliar noise burst into the carriage. Pop. Pop. Pop. Gladys began to tremble. Even though she'd never heard the sound before, she had no doubt it was gunfire, and it was very close. She peered from the train in the direction the soldiers had marched and saw flares of light in the sky.

Gladys no longer felt safe on the train. She had to get off and find shelter. She dropped her suitcases to the ground and climbed off the train. She had to find someone to talk to, but how would anyone understand her? Her heart was thumping hard inside her chest. She looked around and saw a rickety wooden building at the end of a station platform.

Gladys pushed on the door of the small wooden building. The door creaked open. There were no lights inside, but Gladys could make out four men huddled around a small woodstove. Each man held a large mug, and Gladys could smell strong coffee. She recognized three of the men: the engineer from the train, the fireman, and the conductor who had tried so hard to get her off the train in Chita. As soon as Gladys entered the room, the conductor jumped up from his perch on an upturned box and started yelling at her again. She was sure he was saying, "I told you so." Indeed, he had told her so. After several minutes of ranting at Gladys in Russian, he abruptly sat back down and offered her a cup of coffee. She nodded and pulled up one of her suitcases to sit on. She took the mug from the conductor, and for several minutes they all sat in silence, sipping their steaming drinks.

When Gladys had drained her mug of coffee, the conductor launched into a charade like the one he'd acted out back in Chita. This time he had help from the engineer. First, they pointed to the west and made popping noises. Gladys nodded; now she understood—a war was going on down the tracks. Next they pretended to pick up her bags and walk out the door, pointing back up the railroad tracks towards Chita. Gladys understood this, too, but their meaning was like a bad dream to her. Surely they didn't expect her to walk back to Chita. She frowned at them.

The two men then launched into a longer act. They pretended to shoot at each other. Then they dragged each other towards the train. They held up all their fingers several times, and reluctantly Gladys nodded her head. They were telling her the train would stay right where it was until it was filled with wounded soldiers, and only then would it return to Chita.

Gladys tried to think of a way to ask them how long it would be before the train made the return journey. She looked desperately around the room until her eyes fixed on an old yellowed calendar. She began a charade of her own. She rushed over to the calendar and started pointing to the days one at a time. Then she looked at the men and shrugged her shoulders. The engineer nodded, he seemed to understand what she was asking. He held up both hands and flashed all ten fingers. Then he shrugged his shoulders and flashed twenty fingers, and then he shrugged again and flashed thirty fingers. Gladys had her answer. The train could be at the station for ten or twenty or perhaps even thirty days. Gladys didn't have enough supplies with her to last that long, and besides, the men hadn't invited her to stay or offered to share their supplies with her. And why should they? The conductor had done everything in his power, short of picking her up and throwing her off the train in Chita, to prevent her from being here. It was obvious from the way the men acted that they expected her to walk back up the tracks to Chita.

When she could finally see no other course of action, Gladys picked up her two suitcases, stepped off the makeshift station platform, and headed out into the frozen wasteland. The tiny station building soon faded into the night as she followed the snow-covered railroad tracks. Huge pine trees lined both sides of the tracks. Every now and then the sky behind her would light up with the flash of cannon fire. With each flash, Gladys would catch a glimpse of the silhouetted train in the distance. Soon, though, she turned a bend in the tracks and was completely alone. Two weeks earlier she had been standing on the busy platform of Liverpool Street station saying good-bye to all her family and friends. Now she was walking alone in the middle of the night along snow-covered railroad tracks in Siberia. "I want to go to China to serve you, God. Don't let me die here," she prayed over and over with every step she took.

Chapter 4

"It's Missionary, Not Machinery!"

Gladys awoke shivering. She was pulled up into a ball with fresh snow piled on top of her. She was colder than she'd ever been in her life. She had no feeling in her hands or feet. Still, she had awakened. She was alive. She hadn't frozen to death while she slept. She looked around. It was still dark, and for the moment it had stopped snowing. Looking up she could make out the forms of pine trees looming over her. Bit by bit, in her cold, foggy mind, she remembered how she had come to be sleeping in the Siberian snow. Gladys groaned as she stumbled to her frostbitten feet. She fumbled for her two suitcases. She had to keep going. Somehow, she had to make it back to Chita.

The first rays of dawn poked through the trees. Gladys trudged on. The trek seemed to be a little easier in daylight when she could see where she was going. She hoped the sun would provide some much-needed warmth. But as the sun climbed high in the sky, the chill of Siberia seemed to drain the heat from its rays before they reached her. For most of the day, Gladys shivered violently, especially when she had to feel her way through the long railroad tunnels that the icy wind also howled through. In the chilling blackness inside the tunnels, she often wondered what animals might have taken shelter there.

Finally, long after the sun had set, Gladys saw the twinkling lights of Chita far off in the distance. She was going to make it! She wasn't going to die in the Siberian wilderness after all. About two hours later, totally exhausted, Gladys finally climbed onto the railway platform in Chita. She hoped that when people saw how exhausted she was, someone would help her. But no one looked at all interested in a lone women who couldn't speak their language. Finally, Gladys was too tired to care anymore. She arranged her two suitcases on the platform and lay down on them. When the sun came up the next morning, powdery snow that had fallen during the night completely covered Gladys and her bags so that she resembled an abandoned pile of luggage.

The events of the previous two days and nights were like a foggy dream to Gladys. She tried to push herself up with her hands from where she lay, but her hands wouldn't move. They were too cold to do what she wanted them to do.

Gladys lay still, wondering what to do next. People, mainly soldiers, were walking around her, and although she called out, no one seemed to hear her. She tried to focus on a plan of action instead of on the throbbing pain in her frozen fingers and toes and the pangs of hunger that racked her stomach. It seemed so ridiculous to be freezing to death on a station platform in full view of people. It had taken her thirty hours through freezing temperatures to walk back to Chita, and after another night in the exposed cold on the station platform, she needed to get warm, and quickly. To get the help she needed, she had to draw attention to herself. But how was she going to do that?

As Gladys thought about what to do, she saw an important-looking officer in a red cap walking down the platform, and she got an idea. If she could get her leg out from under her coat, she could trip him as he walked by. That would surely get her arrested, which, in turn, would lead to a warm cell. At that moment, nothing mattered more than getting warm, even if it meant getting arrested. Gladys was struggling to free her leg when the red-capped officer signaled to two other soldiers. The three men descended on Gladys. She didn't need to trip the officer after all. The officer waved his hand at Gladys as though he were trying to swat a fly. Gladys got the idea. She was in the way and needed to move from the platform. But where did he expect her to move? Onto the railroad tracks? Into the woodpile? She struggled to sit up, and that, she stubbornly decided, was as far as she would go. She wouldn't move from the platform to die in some forgotten corner of the world. One of the soldiers tried to get her to move, but she shook her head.

Eventually the three men gave up trying to communicate with Gladys. Two of them roughly grabbed her by the arms and dragged her down the platform towards the station building. There they threw her into a tiny room at the side of the building. With a click, the door locked behind her. Gladys had gotten herself arrested, although her "warm" cell wasn't warm at all. The glass in the small window high in the wall was broken, and snow had drifted into the room, forming a mound on the floor. A few sticks of broken furniture were in one corner and a pile of filthy rags in another. But worse than the bitter cold was the stench in the room. It stunk worse than anything Gladys had ever smelled before. It made her sick to her hunger-ravaged stomach. Cold as it was, Gladys stood under the window and tried to avoid the stench by sucking in through her mouth the freezing air that blew in through the shattered glass.

The hours passed slowly, and Gladys wondered what might happen to her next. She also wondered what had become of her bags. How she wished she had her small suitcase with her. She desperately needed something to eat. The gnawing in her stomach was unbearable. The stale cookie she'd eaten a day and a half day before on the trek back to Chita was the last thing she'd eaten. But she didn't have her bag with her, so instead of eating, she reached inside her corset and pulled out her Bible. As she did so, a slip of paper fell from it. Someone had handed the slip to her as she boarded the train in London. She held it up to the fading light coming in through the window. Written on it in bold letters were the words: "Be ye not afraid of them, I am your God (Nehemiah 4 verse 14)." Gladys repeated the verse from the Bible over and over again until she felt her strength returning. She told herself that whatever happened, God would be watching over her.

It was late in the evening when a key finally jangled in the lock. The door swung open, and a soldier walked into the room. He leered at Gladys, then motioned for her to follow him. He led her to another room. At least this room didn't smell. It was also warmer, not because it had any heating but because the windows weren't broken. Gladys stood in front of a long desk. The officer in the red cap and another man sat across the desk. The red-capped officer barked an order to the soldier who had escorted her to the room, and the soldier quickly left. He reappeared again a few moments later holding a mug. He thrust it at Gladys, who took it gratefully and swallowed the strong, luke-warm tea it contained. When the tea hit her empty stomach, it reminded her she hadn't eaten for over two days now.

The red-capped officer barked some more orders, and with cruel smiles on their faces, the two men behind the desk watched as the soldier made Gladys strip to her underclothes. The soldier then made her take off her corset. He chuckled to himself as he found the maze of pockets Gladys's mother had carefully sewn into the garment. Gladys tried not to think about what was happening. Instead, she concentrated on the verse from Nehemiah. At last, the soldier seemed satisfied he'd found all he was going to find and motioned for Gladys to put her clothes back on.

The contents of her pockets lay on the table in front of her. Gladys knew she had to do something and fast. She picked up her passport and waved it at the officer. "British. Me British," she explained, wondering whether she should start singing "God Save the King" to stress the point.

The man seated beside the red-capped officer reached out and took her passport. "I look," he said.

Gladys was relieved—finally, someone who spoke English.

The man studied every page of the passport. "You machinist?" he asked, flipping to the front of her passport.

"No, no," said Gladys. "Not machinist, *missionary.*"

The man looked confused, as if he couldn't hear the difference between the two words.

Gladys looked around, desperate for some way to explain. She saw her Bible and grabbed it. She held it out so he could see it. Then she folded her hands like she was praying and repeated, "Missionary, missionary."

"Yes, machinery. Need good working people, can make machinery go good," he continued, as if he hadn't understood a thing Gladys had been trying to convey to him.

Before Gladys had a chance to say anything further, the red-capped officer abruptly scooped all her belongings, except the Bible, which she was still holding, into a box and marched out of the room. The second man followed right after him. Gladys sat down on a rickety chair and cried. She cried because she was so hungry. She cried because she was so cold. She cried because she had no idea what was going to happen next. Weak and weary, she cried herself to sleep, sitting in the chair with her head resting against the wall.

The next morning she awoke to the prod of a rifle butt. She opened her eyes to see two soldiers standing in front of her. They dragged her to her feet, and then the red-capped officer and his interpreter marched back into the room.

"Machinist good sleeper," smiled the interpreter.

Gladys didn't know whether to correct him or not. The night before he had paid no attention to what she had to say. But before she could decide whether to bother, the interpreter pulled out her passport and pointed to the stamp she had gotten four long days before when she'd unwittingly been on her way to the front line of a war. "Why come back to Chita?" the interpreter demanded.

Gladys tried to explain that she had to come back because of the fighting. But the interpreter wouldn't believe she'd walked back through the snow by herself without help. She tried to make him understand, but in the end she gave up. What difference would it make? He didn't believe anything she said anyway.

After several more minutes of trying to get her to answer their questions, the two men gave up and left the room. They didn't return again until mid-afternoon. By then, Gladys was so hungry she was barely conscious. She had to concentrate hard on what the interpreter was saying to her. He handed back her passport. Inside was a cheaply printed document with seals and stamps all over it. Next he handed her two pieces of cardboard. "This ticket to Nikol'sk-Ussuriyskiy, and then take other train to Pogranichnaya. Train leave now. Go," he said, pointing to the door.

Gladys didn't need to be told twice. She steadied herself before turning and staggering to the door. Outside, her two suitcases were waiting for her. Without looking back, she picked them up, handed the conductor the tickets, and stepped onto the train. As the engine hissed away from the station, she sank into her seat. An old woman sat next to her, and although she smelled of old fish, Gladys inched closer to her for warmth.

It took over an hour of sitting on the train before Gladys had the strength to open her bags. The large suitcase had felt strangely lighter when she'd picked it up. When she flipped open the lid she could see why. All her clothes were gone, except for an old pair of darned stockings her aunt had given her. Gladys clicked open her other suitcase. Thankfully, her spirit stove had been stuffed in there, and the remainder of her food was still there, too. She slumped back in her seat. All she had left was her Bible, the photo of her brother, a pair of darned stockings, her spirit stove, the last of her food, and the English one-pound note she'd been given in The Hague. It was in the only secret pocket the soldier had failed to find in her corset. Everything else she had set out with from London was gone.

As the train rocked and rumbled across the Siberian wilderness, Gladys finally ate her first meal in three days. Never had stale cookies tasted so good!

Of course, Gladys wasn't exactly sure the train was taking her to Nikol'sk-Ussuriyskiy. For all she knew, the whole thing could be a trick to get her to a factory somewhere so she could be the "expert machinist." But the thought of how unmechanical she really was brought a smile to her face in spite of her situation.

The train wound its way eastward, along the border with China. Although it was not a trick, when the train finally arrived at Nikol'sk-Ussuriyskiy, more problems awaited Gladys. An official met her at the train and studied her passport and the paper that had been placed inside it in Chita. She showed him her ticket to Pogranichnaya, where she imagined she would catch another train to Harbin, China. The official shook his head vigorously and took Gladys by the arm. He guided her onto another train and stayed with her until it was ready to leave. As the train gathered speed, Gladys realized they were headed south, but not to China. A fellow passenger, a man with a cage full of chickens, smiled a toothless smile and said, "Vladivostok." The official had put her on a train for Vladivostok, the port city at the end of the railway line across Russia and Siberia. Gladys had no idea what would happen once she got there. And in her worst nightmare, Gladys would never have imagined the ordeal that awaited her in Vladivostok.

It was very late in the afternoon when the train finally pulled into the Vladivostok station. As the passengers got off the train, everyone seemed to have somewhere to go except Gladys. She stood on yet another train station platform wondering what to do next. She scoured the station for clues, and she was rewarded when she saw a poster in English! It was an advertisement for the Intourist Hotel, and although it didn't say exactly where it was, Gladys picked up her bags and headed out the door. She said the name "Intourist Hotel" many times to many different people before someone understood and pointed her in the right direction.

With great relief, Gladys pushed through the revolving door of the hotel. She had hoped the hotel would remind her of home, but it didn't. It was stark and dirty. A clerk beckoned to her, and she walked over to him. As he examined her passport and assigned her a room, the thought struck her that she had no way to pay for it, but she was too exhausted to care. She would worry about that later.

The clerk then waved her towards a short, chunky man with a crumpled uniform. Indeed, the uniform looked as though it hadn't been cleaned for a month. But when she glanced down at her own dirty and torn clothes, Gladys realized she looked every bit as scruffy and unkempt as the man did. She walked over to him, and to her surprise he greeted her in reasonable English. He asked to see her passport and then grunted as he stuffed it into the front pocket of his uniform. Finally, he eased himself up from his chair and told Gladys to follow him. They climbed the stairs, at the top of which he opened the door into a damp and dreary room. The room wasn't heated, but there was a quilt on the bed. The man saluted her, turned around, and headed back downstairs. Gladys closed the door, dropped her bags, and climbed into bed under the warm quilt. She slept late into the following morning.

When she awoke, Gladys looked at herself in the tiny mirror glued to the back of the door. She looked awful. Her face was thin, her hair was matted, and her dress, which she'd slept in, looked even more dirty and crumpled than it had the night before. She opened the door of her room a crack and looked out. To her astonishment, the official who had taken her passport the night before was leaning against the wall in the hallway, smoking a cigarette.

When he saw her, he let out an extra long puff of smoke and said, "I have been waiting to show you around our great city."

"Oh," replied Gladys, not sure what to do next. "I will be ready soon," she said, shutting the door. She sat on the edge of the bed wondering what to do. Who was the man outside the door, and what did he want? Perhaps he wanted money, or the chance to practice his English. Gladys had no way of knowing. So finally she decided to do as he suggested, all the while looking out for clues that might tell her what he wanted.

For Gladys, the tour of the "great city" of Vladivostok was anything but great. The people of the city were thin and poorly dressed. They seemed to look right through Gladys without even seeing her. No one smiled, and the streets were so filled with potholes that Gladys quickly gave up trying to keep her feet dry and instead concentrated on finding the shallowest puddles to wade through. Everything seemed gray and unwashed. Gladys longed to see a splash of color, a flower, a billboard, or a brightly colored coat, anything to relieve the dreariness that surrounded her. She was grateful when finally they rounded a corner, and there in front of her was the Intourist Hotel. She spent the rest of the day in her room.

The following morning, the scene repeated itself. There was the official standing in the hallway waiting for her. Gladys was beginning to feel very uneasy about the whole arrangement. The official had told her the day before he was an interpreter, but the way he followed her every move, he seemed more like a prison guard. Gladys decided she needed some answers. She stepped out of her room and looked the man in the eye. "When do I get to go to Harbin?" she asked in her most commanding voice.

The official narrowed his eyes, and a shrewd smile crossed his face. "What makes you think you are leaving Russia?" he asked.

Gladys's stomach was in knots, but she knew this was no time to panic. She spoke with a low, even voice. "I paid my fare from London to Tientsin, and if your railroad people were honest, they would see that I got there."

"Oh, but you do not need to go to China to work with machines. We have need of machine workers right here," said the official.

Gladys exploded. "It's missionary, not machinery. I have never worked a machine in my life, and I didn't come to Russia to start. I'm going to China," she yelled as she turned and stomped down the stairs.

The gray city of Vladivostok matched her mood as she wandered around. The official was never more than a few feet behind her. As she walked, she prayed. She sensed she was in more danger now than she had been in walking back up the railroad tracks to Chita. The official had her passport, he was the only person she knew who spoke English, her food rations had finally run out that morning, and she had one English pound note to her name. Worst of all, no one back in England knew where she was. She wasn't even supposed to be anywhere near Vladivostok. If she were whisked off to repair machinery in some distant part of Siberia, no one would ever know what had happened to her. And unless she did something soon, Gladys was quite sure she could well end up an unwilling machinist in a Russian factory instead of a missionary in China. The question for her was, how could she get away from the official and from Vladivostok?

Chapter 5

The Knock on the Door

Gladys picked her way through the slimy pud-dles back to the Intourist Hotel. It had been an aimless day of wandering the streets with her "interpreter" close behind. The revolving door of the Intourist Hotel clicked as she pushed on it, and then she heard it click again as the interpreter followed her through the door. Inside the lobby, Gladys glanced around. The interpreter was lighting yet another cigarette and pulling up his chair at the foot of the stairs. Short of crawling out of her second-story window, Gladys could think of no way to escape from him. With her shoulders slumped forward, she climbed the stairs to her room. As she did so, a young girl about seventeen years of age brushed past her. As the girl passed her, Gladys thought she heard her whisper in perfect English, "Don't say anything and follow me." She turned to see whether she was imagining it, but the girl with long, straight black hair was looking the other way. Gladys wondered whether in her desperation to escape she was beginning to imagine things. Her heart beat fast as she turned and followed the girl down the corridor at the top of the stairs. As she rounded a corner in the corridor, Gladys was suddenly grabbed by the sleeve of her orange dress and pulled into a darkened doorway.

"Who are you?" she asked as her eyes adjusted to the shadows.

"That does not matter," whispered the girl. "You are in great danger."

Gladys nodded.

"Your passport?" the girl asked.

"The official has it," replied Gladys.

"You must get it back at all costs," said the girl in an urgent voice. "Look at it carefully. The Communists are desperate for skilled workers. I have seen other foreigners taken to the interior and never heard of again."

A chill ran down Gladys's spine.

"You get your passport," the girl repeated before continuing. "You will hear a knock at your door at midnight. Go with the man quickly. Do not speak to him. Do not look closely at him. Just go fast."

Gladys nodded. She felt as though she were a character in a bad spy novel. Yet it wasn't a story; it was really happening to her.

The girl turned and walked away. With shaking hands, Gladys smoothed a piece of hair that had fallen from her bun. She walked back down the stairs to where the official was sitting in his chair with his hands clasped behind his head and his boots crossed on the table. He didn't bother to move them as Gladys spoke to him.

"You have my passport," she said looking down into his cold eyes. "I need it back now." She spoke in her firmest voice.

"It is still being examined. I will bring it to your room," the official said, and then looking Gladys up and down, he added, "tonight."

Gladys stuffed her hands deep into the pockets of her coat to hide the fact they were shaking violently with fear. What if the two men arrived at her room at the same time? She didn't want to think about it. She turned and climbed the stairs again.

For most of the evening she sat shivering on the edge of the bed with her fur coat tucked around her legs trying to keep warm. Finally, she heard a loud knock on the door. When she opened the door, she saw the official standing in front of her holding a British passport in his right hand. The official stuck his foot in the doorway so that Gladys couldn't shut the door, and then he waved the passport and leered at her. Gladys could see he had more on his mind than just delivering her passport. Quickly, before she even thought about what she was doing, she snatched the passport from the official's hand and threw it back over her head into the room. The surprised official took two steps into the room. He stood so close to Gladys that she could smell the cigarettes on his breath.

"Why did you do that?" he asked in a mocking voice. "I told you I was coming to visit you tonight." He shut the door firmly behind himself.

For a moment Gladys was frozen to the floor with fear. Then she suddenly jumped backwards, screaming, "You can't touch me. You can't touch me. God will protect me."

Her desperation seemed to amuse the official, who laughed heartily. "You forget, you are a woman alone in a strange country. I can do what I like."

Gladys repeated herself. "You can't touch me. God will protect me." As she spoke, the official began to curse her in English. He raised his hand to punch her, but his hand stopped in midair. Instead, as if guided by some invisible force, he turned around, opened the door, and walked out.

Gladys breathed a deep sigh of relief, and with trembling hands quickly bolted the door. She stooped down and picked up her passport. She remembered what the girl had said about examining it. And sure enough, there on the first page of the passport, her occupation had been altered. It no longer read "missionary" but "machinist." It seemed the Russian officials would stop at nothing to get workers for their factories.

More than ever, Gladys knew she had to get away, and quickly. She parted the drapes a little and peered out into the darkness. Ice was already forming on the inside of the window. She was glad to be wearing every piece of clothing she owned, except for the pair of darned stockings. She would have liked to have worn them over her other pair of stockings, but they padded her feet so much she couldn't get her shoes on over them. She had stuffed the old stockings into her coat pocket. For no particular reason, she had also taken the English one-pound note out of the secret pocket in her corset and slipped it into her coat pocket along with the stockings.

Midnight came and went, but there was no knock on her door. She began to worry. Had something gone wrong? Had the girl lied? Was it all an elaborate trap? Maybe it was a sick joke someone was playing on her. Almost two hours passed before the knock on her door finally came. It was so soft Gladys wasn't sure whether it was real or not. She tiptoed to the door and unbolted it. She knew she was taking a risk. It could just as easily be the official again, but she had no choice. It wasn't safe for her to stay any longer in Vladivostok. She would just have to trust that a pair of total strangers were willing to risk their lives to save hers.

The door swung open, and there stood a tall man in an old overcoat with his hat pulled down over his face. He put his finger to his lips and motioned for Gladys to follow him. Gladys pulled on her thick woolen gloves, grabbed her two bags, and crept out the door. The man with the overcoat led her along the hallway and then down the stairs.

Gladys's heart began to race. The man was leading her right out the front entrance of the hotel past the clerk and the official. She prayed a silent prayer and then listened. She heard snoring coming from the clerk's desk, and as she got to the bottom of the stairs, she saw that the official's chair was empty. Gladys gripped her suitcases hard until her fingers ached, and she kept walking. The revolving door squeaked as she went through it. The clerk's snoring faltered at the noise, but then it resumed.

At last, Gladys was out on the pitch-black street without the official following her. Other than the light from the hotel lobby, not a light was to be seen. After leaving the glow of the hotel lobby, Gladys had to squint to see the man in front of her. She and the man stayed close to the sides of buildings as they walked. Gladys stumbled through potholes, wondering where she was going. Slowly, as she began to adjust to the situation, she noticed some clues. There was a salty smell in the air, like the smell of the dock in Hull where she'd caught the boat to Holland three weeks before. On the skyline in the distance she could make out some tall, thin towers, far too thin to be buildings. Gladys was sure they were headed towards the docks and guessed that the towers were cranes. Was she about to be put on a ship to China instead of on a train? She didn't care, as long as whatever it was took her away from the danger she was in.

Gladys stumbled on over railway lines and into a large paved area. Packing cases were stacked everywhere, and from behind one packing case emerged the girl from the hotel with the long black hair. Gladys walked towards her. When she looked back, the man in the overcoat was fading into the shadows of the night. Gladys wanted to thank him, but she knew she dare not call out to him. Within seconds he was gone. Gladys turned back to the girl.

"You made it," the girl said with admiration.

"Yes," replied Gladys. "Why are you helping me?"

"When we are able, we help those who need help," was the girl's reply. Then she went on. "But now I can do no more for you. You must take the next step alone. See that freighter over there?" She pointed towards the dark outline of a ship in the distance.

Gladys nodded.

"It is a Japanese ship," she went on. "It sails at dawn for Tsuruga, Japan, and you must be on it. No matter what, you must be on it."

"But I don't have any money for the fare," interrupted Gladys.

The girl looked her straight in the eye. "Beg the captain, do whatever you have to do, but get on that ship. It is your only hope."

Gladys nodded again.

"The captain of the ship is in that hut over there. You must make him take you with him." The girl pointed to a ramshackle wooden hut in the direction of the ship just beyond the stacks of packing crates.

A little frightened, Gladys knew what she had to do. She reached for the young girl's bare hands. "You've saved my life, and I have nothing to give you," she said. Then she had an idea. She stripped off her woolen gloves and handed them to the girl. Then she took the old pair of stockings from her coat pocket and handed them over as well. "They're not much, but they're all I have."

The girl nodded and smiled and then nudged Gladys toward the hut. "Good luck," she said as she turned and slipped away into the shadows.

The single lightbulb that lit the inside of the hut blinded Gladys's eyes for a moment as she walked in out of the darkness. As her eyes adjusted, she saw four Japanese men playing cards around a makeshift table.

Gladys took a deep breath. "I need to talk to the captain of the freighter," she said.

The man closest to her stood up and in good English said, "What can I do for you?"

"I must get on your ship," said Gladys frantically.

The captain looked at her fur overcoat with no sleeves, her crumpled orange dress, filthy shoes, and gloveless hands and asked whether she had money to pay for the trip.

"No, I have nothing. But you must let me on your ship. You must. I'm a British citizen, and I must get away from here," begged Gladys, thrusting her passport at him.

The captain flicked through it. "You have nothing of value at all?" he questioned. "No jewelry, no watch, no money?"

Gladys shook her head. She had forgotten about the one-pound note in her pocket. Anyway, it was such a small amount it wouldn't have bought her passage on a ship. She held her breath and waited for what he would say next.

"A British citizen in trouble," he said. "We cannot have that. But I cannot take you as a passenger if you can't pay."

Gladys's heart sank.

"But," continued the captain, a little smile on his lips, "a prisoner, I could take you as a prisoner, and then you would be under my protection. I would have to hand you over to the British authorities in Tsuruga. Would that do?" he asked kindly.

Tears of relief welled in Gladys's eyes. "Yes, yes," she enthusiastically replied, wiping her eyes with the back of her hand. "I will gladly be your prisoner. Anything is better than staying here."

The captain reached into the satchel he had with him and pulled out a sheet of paper. "Please sign the form, and then we will go."

Gladys couldn't read a word of what she signed. It was all written in Japanese, but somehow she trusted the captain. As soon as the paper was signed, the four men rose from the table and headed into the darkness. Gladys gratefully followed them.

They reached the pier where the freighter was

moored, and the sailors jumped aboard. There was only a foot-and-a-half gap between the ship and the pier. Instead of jumping straight aboard as the sailors had, Gladys put her bags down for a moment to take a deep breath before she jumped. It was a bad decision. Suddenly, Gladys heard the sound of jackboots running on cobblestones. She grabbed her bags, but it was too late. Six large Russian soldiers surrounded her and towered over her. She looked to the ship for help; the sailors watched, but they did not move. She was still on Russian soil, and she supposed the sailors dared not interfere with the soldiers.

Gladys had to think fast. Suddenly, she remembered the pound note in her coat pocket. She spun around and threw her bags onto the ship. Quickly, she pulled the pound note from her coat pocket, waved it in the air, and then let it go. As it fluttered to the ground, six pairs of eyes focused on it, and six pairs of hands grasped for it. While the soldiers' attention was momentarily diverted, Gladys jumped aboard ship and began running up the stairway towards the captain on the bridge. The soldiers yelled at her, but it was too late. The captain had given the order to cast off, and the freighter began to drift away from the dock before the soldiers could do anything. Gladys was safe. She was headed for Japan and away from Russia.

Another passenger—a German woman—was onboard with Gladys. The two women swapped stories of their perilous journeys through Russia.

The German woman's hands were bandaged, and she unwrapped them to show Gladys. The skin had been peeled back on several of her fingers, and Gladys could see muscles and even parts of bone underneath. She couldn't imagine how the woman could have injured herself in such a way. Then she heard the story of what had happened. The German woman had been robbed by a mob of Russian men. Everything, including her luggage, money, coat, gloves, and scarf had been stolen. The robbers also demanded the rings the woman had been wearing. When she hesitated, they ripped them off, tearing skin and flesh from her fingers. After hearing the woman's story, Gladys was even more grateful to know that every turn of the ship's propeller was taking her farther away from the Communist nightmare she had just traveled through.

Things went much better for Gladys when she reached Tsuruga, a small port on Japan's west coast. The captain of the ship personally handed his "prisoner" over to an official from the British consulate who brought Gladys a huge meal and paid for her train ticket to Kobe, though not before telling her he thought she was crazy. In Kobe, Gladys found a missionary compound and was welcomed inside. She had a wonderful hot bath and slept in a comfortable bed for the first time since leaving London. While she slept, one of the missionaries took the unused part of her train ticket from Chita to Harbin and traded it for a boat trip to Tientsin. And so on Saturday, November 5, 1930, twenty-one days after leaving London for China, Gladys began the final leg of her journey on a steamship.

As the ship weaved its way through the southern islands of Japan and then steamed out across the Yellow Sea, Gladys thanked God that the journey was nearly over. In Tientsin, Mrs. Lawson would be waiting for her. Soon she would finally be able to begin her missionary work in China.

Little did Gladys know that Mrs. Lawson had not seriously expected a housemaid from London to actually make it all the way to China, and Mrs. Lawson was nowhere near Tientsin. If Gladys wanted to work with Mrs. Lawson, she was going to have to find her first.

Chapter 6

The Road Ends Here

Gladys felt the color drain from her face. "How long would that take?" she stammered to ask the principal of the Anglo-Chinese College in Tientsin. She had just been told that Mrs. Lawson hadn't been in Tientsin for quite some time, and the last anyone had heard of her, she was to the west in the town of Tsechow in Shansi province. Gladys wanted to burst into tears. Everything about her journey was turning out to be a hundred times harder than she'd imagined.

The principal, a short man with a balding head, smiled kindly at her. "It's quite a journey to Tsechow, but a very pretty one. First you must travel one hundred miles by train to Peking, and then take another train about two hundred and fifty miles southwest to Yutsu, where the railway ends. From there you'll have to take buses south until you reach Tsechow. All in all, it will take you a day to get to Peking, three more to Yutsu, and perhaps another fifteen to twenty days by bus to get to Tsechow."

Gladys echoed, "Fifteen to twenty days?" She was too stunned to ask anything else. She'd traveled for three weeks to get to Tientsin, only to find out she still had another three or more weeks of traveling ahead of her before she reached Mrs. Lawson. She was barely halfway through her journey! Her shoulders slumped forward, and she slid into a nearby chair, thinking about all she'd been through to get this far and what might lie ahead for her.

The missionaries in Tientsin were kind to Gladys, who spent several days with them, resting from her trip across Russia and Siberia and eating every bit of food they gave her. The missionaries also gave her the money she needed for the last leg of her journey. They understood her disappointment, and they encouraged her to go on and find Mrs. Lawson. Virtually no Christians lived in the part of China that Mrs. Lawson had gone to, and missionaries were much needed in that region. Not only that, since Mrs. Lawson had lived in China for nearly fifty years, there was a lot Gladys could learn from her about being a missionary to the Chinese.

Three days after arriving in Tientsin by ship, Gladys felt strong enough to continue her journey.

She was grateful for all that the local missionaries had done for her. They had even located a Christian businessman, Mr. Lu, who was traveling in the same direction and would escort Gladys most of the way to Tsechow. Wearing her freshly washed clothes, and with her suitcase restocked with tea and bags of rice and noodles, Gladys set out to find Mrs. Lawson.

Mr. Lu was a wonderful traveling companion. He spoke good English, and he explained a lot of the history of China to Gladys as they went along. At school, Gladys had finished at the bottom of her history class. But what Mr. Lu was explaining to her wasn't dusty history from a school textbook. As they rolled past pagodas and temples, villages and neatly cultivated rice fields, the history Gladys was hearing about seemed to come alive right before her eyes.

In the distance, Mr. Lu pointed out the mountains that the Great Wall of China ran along. He explained that the Great Wall was built to keep out the Tartars. Well, not really the Tartars themselves, but their horses. He explained that men could climb over the wall, but there was no way to get a horse over it. When the Tartars had to leave their horses on one side and go on without them, they were not nearly as strong or invincible as they had been with their horses. Mr. Lu tried to be polite as he explained that China had always fought to keep foreigners out, and Chinese people, especially those who lived in the country, still thought foreigners were devils. Gladys laughed nervously as he told her this. She wondered how anyone could think of her as a devil. She would find out soon enough.

So far in her journey from London, Gladys had stayed in a hotel only once, the dreaded Intourist Hotel in Vladivostok. For the rest of the journey, she had slept either on the train, on the station platform, or with other missionaries. But after they left the train in Yutsu and began the bone-jarring bus trip to Tsechow, Gladys and Mr. Lu had to find a place to sleep each night. It wasn't difficult to find somewhere to sleep. Chinese people seemed to be on the move all the time, so there were many inns along the way. But these inns were not like any inns Gladys had stayed in before. They weren't inns with bedrooms, closets, curtains, and beds. Chinese inns were quite different. They were one large square room, bare except for a long, low platform made from bricks in the middle or along one wall of the room. The platform was called a k'ang, and it was heated from underneath by a fire. The k'ang, as Gladys found out on her first night in one of the inns, was a communal bed. Men, women, and children, strangers and traveling companions, officials and peasants, all slept side by side on the platform.

The first night sleeping on a k'ang was very strange for Gladys. For one thing, she slept fully dressed, like everyone else. Mr. Lu said it offered protection against a neighboring sleeper's lice or fleas. He also pointed out that there was nowhere to take off your clothes and put on pajamas and nowhere to protect clothes from being stolen while a person slept. Once again, Gladys used her sleeveless fur coat as a blanket. Even so, it was hard for someone used to sleeping on a mattress to get used to sleeping on bricks. And then there was the snoring and snuffling. The old woman beside Gladys kept trying to roll over on her, and Mr. Lu made peculiar sucking noises when he lay on his back. Another man, three bodies down, had a cage with five chickens in it that he placed next to his head. The chickens scratched and squawked while their owner slept soundly. As the night slowly passed, Gladys could only imagine what people back in England would think if they could see her at that moment.

Finally dawn came, and the sleepers began to stir. Gladys sat up. Every one of her bones ached as she crawled to the edge of the k'ang and pulled her shoes from her coat pocket. She noticed the old woman beside her staring at her feet. The toe of her stocking had a hole in it, but Gladys didn't think that was what the woman was looking at. When Gladys looked down at the old woman's feet, she saw, to her horror, that the feet were deformed, wrapped in bandages and only about half the length of a normal foot but twice as thick. The woman's feet looked more like horse hooves than feet. Gladys knew why. The missionaries in Tientsin had told her that Chinese people considered tiny feet to be beautiful and that a Chinese woman would never find a husband if she had "huge" feet like Europeans. So in China, it was traditional for the women to have their feet bound when they were babies so that the front of each foot would fold over and grow back under the rest of the foot.

Though she'd heard about the practice, this was the first time Gladys had seen it up close. And what she saw looked grotesque. She wondered how anybody could think it pretty or desirable. She watched the old woman stand up and move across the room and out the door in small, hobbled footsteps.

Each morning, Mr. Lu and Gladys ate the same breakfast of soup made with noodles and vegetables. After breakfast, they climbed onto yet another bus and continued their journey. It was the same pattern day after day—travel by day and sleep in an inn by night. Each day the buses lurched over rocky outcrops, forded swift-flowing streams, and stopped for the endless repairs the drivers had to make on the decrepit buses.

The principal at the Anglo-Chinese school in Tientsin, though, had been wrong. It didn't take fifteen to twenty days of bus travel to reach Tsechow. It took twenty-five days! And Gladys had enough bruises from the bumpy trip to account for every one of those days.

After Mr. Lu reached his destination, Gladys had to travel on alone for the last two days. But before they parted company, Mr. Lu had taught Gladys a few simple words in Chinese, including the word for "mission." So when the bus finally screeched to a halt in Tsechow, Gladys climbed out of it and approached the first person she saw. She repeated in Chinese the word *mission* in the same singsong way Mr. Lu had taught her to say it, and much to her delight, the man seemed to understand. He pointed up a hill while making motions to go to the left. All the while, he rattled on in Chinese. Gladys smiled a thank you at him, picked up her suitcases, and began the final climb to meet Mrs. Lawson.

Gladys was greeted at the door of the mission house by an old woman. She reached out and shook the woman's hand. "Mrs. Lawson," she began with tremendous relief, "I'm Gladys Aylward from London."

The old woman smiled sweetly. At the same time, she shook her head. "You're mistaken, my dear," she said. "I'm Mrs. Smith. Mrs. Lawson isn't here. Come in and have a cup of tea and tell me how you got here."

Over several cups of strong black tea the details of Gladys's trip from London to Tsechow came tumbling out. Mrs. Smith's eyes were wide with amazement at Gladys's tale. When Gladys came to the part of the story about Vladivostok and the Russian official, Mrs. Smith reached out and held Gladys's hand. When Gladys had finished recounting her adventures, Mrs. Smith told her about Mrs. Lawson. It was true Mrs. Lawson had been in Tsechow, but that was several months ago. Mrs. Lawson had moved on, and as far as Mrs. Smith knew, she was staying in a little walled town called

Yangcheng, high up in the mountains, two days' journey away.

Again, Gladys could hardly believe what she was hearing. She still had another two days of travel to get to Mrs. Lawson. "May I stay with you tonight?" she asked wearily. "In the morning I will take the bus to Yangcheng."

"You can stay here as long as you like, my dear," said Mrs. Smith kindly. "However, you cannot catch a bus to Yangcheng."

"Why not?" asked Gladys.

"I'm afraid the road ends here," replied Mrs. Smith.

Gladys felt the urge to giggle. It was all too much to take in at once. "What do you mean the road ends here?" she asked. "How did Mrs. Lawson get to Yangcheng?"

"From here to Yangcheng there is only a mule track. It's quite steep, and only the guides and the mules are safe walking it. Everyone else must travel on a mule litter."

The next morning Gladys found out what a mule litter was. The muleteer, who would lead the mule train into the mountains, chuckled as he helped Gladys climb into the basket that was perched on the back of one of his eight mules. Gladys's suitcases were slung over another mule. Finally, the muleteer barked a command, and the mule train began to move. Gladys's entire body shuddered and jerked with every step the mule took. She gripped the low sides of the litter basket with both hands in an attempt to cushion the jolts, but it didn't seem to help much.

To try to take her mind off the harsh ride, Gladys prayed. She thanked God for getting her safely this far and for Mrs. Smith, who had been so kind to her, even giving her the padded blue trousers and jacket that she was now wearing and that made her look like everyone else in this part of China. Gladys also prayed that Mrs. Lawson would be at Yangcheng when she got there, because she didn't know what she would do if Mrs. Lawson weren't there. Mrs. Smith had told her that Yangcheng was a town where there was not another Christian, and most people there had never seen a white person other than Mrs. Lawson. Gladys had also paid the last of her money for the mule ride to Yangcheng. If Mrs. Lawson weren't there, Gladys would be stranded in a place where no one spoke English and where everyone would think she was a foreign devil. The thought terrified her.

In the distance Gladys could see tall mountains. Mrs. Smith had told her they would travel over gently rolling hills for about nine miles and then start to climb up into the mountains. The mule litter was following a thousand-year-old trail through the mountains. Walled mountain villages were strung like beads along the trail. Mrs. Smith had said that because the villages were a day's journey apart, the mule trains had to find shelter each evening. They dared not travel at night because of the danger from robbers and wolves that lurked in the area. The muleteers needed the safety of a village with walls and locked gates in which to spend the night.

The sun was beginning to set over the western horizon as they hurried through the gates at Chowtsun. A single path wound up between the houses, and Gladys watched in astonishment as the lead mule walked past many open gates until it came to one that led into a wide courtyard. No one had led it there, but somehow the mule knew exactly where it should go. A Chinese woman hobbled from the house and yelled what Gladys presumed was a greeting. It must have been, because the whole mule train crowded into the courtyard, and the gates were shut behind them.

That night Gladys slept on the k'ang along with the muleteers. She spent a good part of the night thinking about meeting Mrs. Lawson the next day. She hoped Mrs. Lawson would be as kind and motherly as Mrs. Smith had been. After her long and exhausting journey, Gladys was beginning to feel the need for some loving attention.

In the morning, Gladys couldn't decide whether she was stiffer from the mule litter the day before or from another night sleeping on a k'ang. The head muleteer had snored loudly all night, and Gladys couldn't wait to be in her own bed in her own room in Mrs. Lawson's mission house by evening.

It was a seven-hour trip to Yangcheng, and Gladys's body ached more with every step the mule took. They were high in the mountains now, and the mules were often clomping along over razor-edged rocks that formed the trail. Gladys spent a lot of time looking up enjoying the sky and the occasional eagle that circled above. She tried to avoid looking down at the valley floor hundreds of feet straight below the narrow trail they were making their way along.

As they rounded a sharp corner in the trail, the mule train came to a halt. The head muleteer trotted over to Gladys, who knew he didn't know a single word of English. As Gladys wondered what he might want, he lifted a callused finger and pointed to the southwest. He said only one word, but it was the one word Gladys wanted to hear at that moment more than any other word: Yangcheng.

Gladys followed the direction of the man's finger, and sure enough, rising in the distance was a village that looked just like a picture of Cinderella's castle that Gladys had seen in a fairy tale book. Jutting straight out of the rocks was a high wall, and peeking over the wall were the most fantastically shaped roofs Gladys had ever seen. The roofs had turrets and spheres, cones and towers, and Gladys gasped at their beauty.

As the mule train got closer, Yangcheng became even more beautiful. At last they entered through the east gate of the town. This time the muleteer held the lead mule's bit firmly. He stopped to talk to a man who was squatting in the late afternoon sun. Gladys supposed he was asking directions to Mrs. Lawson's house. Sure enough, the muleteer led them down a narrow path to the left. Several hundred yards along the path, they stopped in front of what looked like an abandoned old building. One of the balconies was falling down, and the doors to the building had all been ripped off by their hinges and were nowhere to be seen. In the doorway stood a stark, white-haired old woman, dressed in blue trousers and jacket. The woman picked her way over the bricks and trash that lay around the courtyard and stared at Gladys. "Who are you?" she asked with an abrupt Scottish accent.

"I'm Gladys Aylward," offered Gladys wearily. "Are you Mrs. Lawson?'

"Yes, of course I am," she replied, eyeing Gladys with her piercing blue eyes. "You'd better come in, then," she added matter-of-factly.

Gladys climbed down from her perch on the mule, picked up her bags, which the muleteer had deposited on the cobblestones beside her, and followed Mrs. Lawson into the dilapidated building, wondering as she did so what she'd gotten herself into this time.

Chapter 7

Inn of Eight Happinesses

Mrs. Lawson led Gladys across the courtyard, down a passage, and into a large room. There was a k'ang along one wall, and several wooden boxes fashioned into a table and chairs were along the other. Mrs. Lawson motioned for Gladys to sit down and called out something in Chinese. In response, an old Chinese man bustled into the room. Mrs. Lawson introduced him to Gladys as Yang, the cook. Yang smiled a toothless smile at Gladys and then listened to the instructions Mrs. Lawson gave him in Chinese. When she had finished, Yang bowed and left the room.

Mrs. Lawson explained that she had rented the big house for two years. The people of Yangcheng thought it was haunted, and no one had been in it for years. Of course, being "haunted" meant she had been able to rent it very cheaply. Gladys smiled as best she could, but the place was nothing at all like the homey, comfortable house she'd imagined. And Mrs. Lawson wasn't the sweet old lady she'd expected. Mrs. Lawson barked out questions and then didn't bother to wait for a reply.

Gladys was wishing Mrs. Lawson were more like Mrs. Smith in Tsechow, when Yang reappeared with a steaming bowl of noodles and vegetables. Gladys gulped the soup down. In her excitement to get to Yangcheng, she'd forgotten just how hungry she was. After enjoying two bowls of soup, she cleared her throat. "Where would you like me to put my things and sleep tonight?" she asked.

"Anywhere you can find. I don't care. One room is as messy as the next, and none of them have doors," Mrs. Lawson replied.

Gladys picked up her bags and wandered around the house. The rooms on the second floor had balconies that overlooked the courtyard below, although the view wasn't scenic. In the end, Gladys settled on a downstairs room that had more junk in it than most of the other rooms but didn't smell as bad.

After choosing a room and putting her bags away, Gladys decided to stretch her legs and take a short walk around her new neighborhood. She slipped through the gateway and out into the narrow street where the muleteer had let her off less than an hour before. Farther down the street, a group of women carrying water jars stopped to stare at Gladys, who waved to them. Suddenly, without even talking to one another, each of the women put down her jar, picked up clods of mud and dirt, and hurled them at Gladys. Some little children ran from a nearby courtyard and giggled with delight at what was happening.

Gladys turned and fled, clods of mud thudding against the back of her pants as she ran. Once she was safely inside the courtyard of Mrs. Lawson's house, she burst into tears. Mrs. Lawson came out to see what the commotion was and instructed Gladys to come inside. It would not do to have her crying where people could see.

"What's the matter?" she asked, once they were inside.

"It's the people out there," sobbed Gladys, as she wiped clumps of mud from her pants. "The women threw mud at me, and then the children laughed at me. How will I ever tell them about the gospel message if they won't let me come near them?"

Mrs. Lawson frowned a little. "Getting upset about it won't help, though I must admit in all my fifty-three years in China I've never seen a less friendly group than the people of Yangcheng. But you're so lucky," she went on. "You have black hair and brown eyes like they do. Imagine how much they fear me with my white hair and blue eyes."

Gladys nodded. She hadn't thought about how it must be for Mrs. Lawson. The hair of older Chinese people sometimes went a little gray, but never snow-white like Mrs. Lawson's.

"They call us *lao-yang-kwei*, foreign devil. But we must get used to that. Think of it as a challenge. We have to work out some way to reach these people with the gospel message. God has given us a difficult task," said Mrs. Lawson, then adding briskly, "but not an impossible task."

Gladys wiped her eyes. It was a challenge she wasn't sure she was up to, but she would try her best to keep going.

The weeks began to roll by. For Gladys the time was filled with cleaning up the house and having language lessons with Yang, who was teaching her the local Yangcheng dialect of Chinese. Yang was a very patient tutor, and Gladys spent a lot of time in the kitchen with him. Most evenings she would also take a stroll with Mrs. Lawson. Gradually, the people of Yangcheng began to accept the sight of the two foreign women. The women were still jeered at, and sometimes spat on, but after several weeks, the mud throwing stopped.

It was on one of her walks that Gladys saw something she would never forget. As she stepped from the courtyard, she noticed the street was empty. There were no children playing, no old women gossiping, and no street peddlers selling their wares. She was wondering where everyone could be, when she heard a cheer go up from the direction of the marketplace. Gladys hurried toward the sound of the cheering. Only the week before she had seen a performing bear in the marketplace, and Mrs. Lawson had told her that jugglers and acrobats often traveled through the area and performed there. Sometimes the crowd would throw money, small copper coins worth a fraction of a penny, at the performers' feet as payment. As Gladys rounded the corner, she saw a huge crowd gathered. She hoped the entertainment hadn't started yet.

Gladys was trying to angle into a position where she could see over the crowd, when she felt someone grab her hand. She looked around, straight into the eyes of the woman who lived next door. Gladys smiled at her, amazed by her friendliness. The woman dragged Gladys to the front of the crowd just as a hush fell over the crowd. Gladys caught her breath and looked around. There were no bears, no traveling acrobats or jugglers, just a single man kneeling on the cobblestones with his head down. Beside him stood one of the mandarin's soldiers. But what was all the fuss about? Gladys had no idea.

Suddenly, the soldier reached for the long curved sword hanging at his waist. With a single action, he pulled the sword from his belt and lifted it high above the kneeling man's head. Another roar went up from the crowd, and in a sickening instant, Gladys understood what was happening. She had a front-row seat to an execution. Before she could turn away, the sword had swished through the air. The kneeling man's head fell to the ground, rolled

several times, and stopped face up at Gladys's feet.
Another roar went up from the crowd. Gladys held
her hand over her mouth as she pushed her way
through the crowd. She thought she was going to be
sick. She had to get away from the scene. She ran all
the way back to the house. Inside Mrs. Lawson was
writing in her journal. She looked up when Gladys
came rushing into the room, sat down on the nearest box, and broke into sobs.

"What's the matter this time?" she asked.

"They killed a man, right in the marketplace,
right where I was standing," wailed Gladys.

"So you saw an execution, did you?" said Mrs.
Lawson, calmly.

"Yes," stammered Gladys. "And the worst thing
was everyone watching and then cheering. It was
horrible. Horrible. How could they do that?"

Mrs. Lawson sighed. "You're in China now, not
England. Here public executions are common.
They'll display the head on the top of the wall.
Sometimes there will be ten or twenty of them lined
up in a row. The body will be thrown over the city
wall into the ravine. Of course, there's a procedure.
They don't just kill anyone. There would have been
a trial. The mandarin would have found the man
guilty of some crime, most likely robbery, and sentenced him to death. It is the Chinese way, and we
must accept it."

"But the crowd loved it. Little children watched.
How could they do that?" asked Gladys, still sob-
bing.

"It wasn't too long ago that public executions were carried out in England," Mrs. Lawson pointed out. "All people are capable of taking pleasure in the pain of others. We must accept things as they are and work hard to bring change through sharing the gospel message. That's the only way they will understand the sadness of a wasted human life. In the meantime, go and wash your face. Crying never helped anyone."

With that, the conversation was over, and Mrs. Lawson returned to writing in her journal.

Gladys never mentioned the incident again to Mrs. Lawson. She didn't want another lecture, no matter how true what Mrs. Lawson said might be. She wished Mrs. Lawson were a little more motherly, but Gladys decided that at seventy-four years of age, Mrs. Lawson wasn't likely to change, so Gladys had just better get used to the old woman's gruffness.

About this time, Gladys began to doubt whether they would ever be able to find a way to talk meaningfully with the townspeople. Even though the two of them were now tolerated, no one was interested in attending a Bible study or any other such activity the women offered. Something had to change, but neither woman was sure what it was, that is, until they went for one of their late afternoon walks together.

Gladys loved to look out over the city wall and watch the last few straggling mule trains wind their way up to the village. She'd already decided that one day she would to go to the end of the trail and back with a mule train. "Just think of the possibilities," she said, unaware that she was thinking out loud.

"Of what?" asked Mrs. Lawson.

"Of traveling with a mule train," she said dreamily. "All those little towns like Yangcheng, where they stop each night. If a muleteer were a Christian, he could spread the gospel message to so many people who have never heard it before. It would be so effortless."

Mrs. Lawson grabbed Gladys's arm and swung her around so they faced each other. "That's it. That's it. Why didn't I see it before?" she said excitedly.

"See what?" asked Gladys, not following the conversation.

"We'll turn this house into an inn," exclaimed Mrs. Lawson.

Gladys wasn't used to seeing Mrs. Lawson excited about anything. "An inn?" she echoed.

"Yes. It's the perfect answer. We can't get the people into a church, but we can get them into an inn, especially if it's the cleanest inn on the whole trail."

Gladys nodded, thinking back on her own mule trip. She would like to have stayed at an inn without lice and fleas. "But we didn't come to be innkeepers, did we?" she asked, a little unsure of what exactly Mrs. Lawson had in mind for them.

"Don't you see it?" Mrs. Lawson was becoming a little impatient. "We get the muleteers in. We water the mules, feed the men a good meal, and then offer them something no other inn does." She pursed her lips for a moment, apparently waiting for Gladys to appreciate the full impact of what she was about to say. "Then I tell them Bible stories for free. They'll love it. All Chinese people love entertainment. Noah, Moses, Jesus, Paul—they'll love the stories. And you mark my words, those stories will be told and retold all along the trail. Only God knows how many people could hear about the gospel as a result of our inn."

Mrs. Lawson stopped and folded her hands. Gladys was surprised. Mrs. Lawson spoke as though the inn were already up and running, and not a leaky old house with broken windows, missing doors, and no coal for the k'ang. Still, as Gladys looked back down at the last mule train hurrying to reach Yangcheng before the sun disappeared completely, a thrill came over her. This was a project she could throw herself into.

The next few weeks were busy and happy ones for Gladys and Mrs. Lawson as they worked together turning the house into an inn. There was repair work to be done, millet and vegetables to be purchased, coal to be ordered, and the courtyard made into a mule stable. Thankfully, Mrs. Lawson had a small income that provided enough money to make the repairs and buy the provisions. The women calculated that when the inn was running, it would pay for itself and provide enough money to pay Yang, while leaving a small amount for extras.

All the inns along the trail had rather grand sounding names, and Gladys and Mrs. Lawson decided that their inn needed a grand name as well. So they called it the "Inn of Eight Happinesses." The name had no special meaning; Mrs. Lawson just liked the sound of it.

The Inn of Eight Happinesses quickly took shape. As she worked away, Gladys wondered what she would be responsible for once it opened. Yang would be preparing the meals and serving them to the muleteers. Mrs. Lawson would be telling Bible stories after the meal and keeping track of the finances. That left one other responsibility: the mules. Someone had to take care of them. The mules needed to have the mud scraped off their legs and be fed and watered each night. Gladys had a suspicion that she would be that someone.

Sure enough, she was. She also had one other job. Somehow she had to get the muleteers into the inn. "Muyo beatch. Muyo goodso. How. How. How. Lai. Lai. Lai." Gladys said the words over and over to herself a hundred times to make sure she remembered them. Yang told her the words meant, "We have no bugs. We have no fleas. Good. Good. Good. Come. Come. Come." But as many times as Gladys repeated the words to herself, she still couldn't imagine actually standing in the street yelling them to muleteers. But then, neither could she see herself scraping the mud off the mules. She'd never cared for an animal bigger than a cat! Still, she told herself, if the muleteers were inside the Inn of Eight

Happinesses listening to Bible stories, she would do her best in the stable to keep the mules happy.

Gladys stood and shouted until she was hoarse the first night the inn was open. But nothing happened. Not a single muleteer stopped for the night. When the last mule train had passed by, Gladys walked back inside. The inn looked so beautiful. The table was set and ready for the bowls of delicious noodle soup Yang had made. Mrs. Lawson's Bible lay open on her chair, ready for her to tell stories after dinner. The k'ang had been scrubbed, and a warm fire was radiating from under it.

Gladys stood in the doorway and shook her head. "I'm sorry," she offered. "No matter what I did, the muleteers wouldn't stop."

"Tomorrow you'll have to *make* them come in," said Mrs. Lawson firmly.

"Make them?" quizzed Gladys. "I did everything I could."

"Well, not exactly. Tomorrow you'll have to grab the mules by the bridle and pull them in. Once they're in the courtyard, nothing on earth will move them." Mrs. Lawson spoke with such finality that Gladys didn't argue.

All the next day, Gladys worried about getting the muleteers to stop. She discussed it with Yang, in limited Yangcheng dialect, of course, since he spoke no English, and by the time the sun began to set, she felt ready to try again.

Gladys stood in the shadows outside the inn as the mule trains passed by. She let the first two go past as she got up her courage. When she heard the steady clip-clop of the third mule train, she waited silently for the lead mule to come level with her hiding place. At what she thought was the right moment, she leaped from her hiding place and reached for the mule's bridle. However, she'd misjudged her timing and ended up reaching for the head muleteer instead. He screamed with surprise. The other five muleteers scattered into the shadows, but the head muleteer couldn't flee because the reins were tightly wound around his hand.

Gladys knew she had to lead the mules into the courtyard, and fast, before the muleteer realized what she was doing. She rushed to the lead mule and stood in front of him. The mule lowered his head and pushed it into her stomach. He lifted Gladys high into the air and bolted into the courtyard. Mrs. Lawson and Yang arrived at the doorway just in time to see the mule dump Gladys onto the cobblestones.

"Well done, Gladys," congratulated Mrs. Lawson, looking at the mule train standing in the courtyard. "However you did it doesn't matter now. We have our first guest."

But not for long. The head muleteer took one look at Mrs. Lawson with her white hair, unwound the reins from his hand, and fled through the gate.

"What do we do now?" asked Gladys, picking herself up off the cobblestones.

Mrs. Lawson spoke to Yang. They talked much too fast for Gladys to understand what they were saying. Then she turned and said, "Yang says not to worry. This is a good start. The mules and their loads are worth far too much money to abandon. Yang will go and find the muleteers. They will come back with him. They have to; we have their mules. Yang will tell them they are safe staying here. They'll quickly find out we're nothing to be scared of."

Gladys nodded. It was all turning out to be so much more complicated than she'd imagined it would be. She hoped that after tonight, things would get a little easier, but she had no idea of the problems that lay ahead.

Chapter 8

Jesus in the Ark

A nd then," continued Yang in his most dramatic voice, "Jesus opened the door and let all the animals in two by two."

Gladys frowned. She'd just come in from brushing down the mules and had stopped to listen to Yang tell a Bible story to the muleteers.

"After forty long, long days and forty long, long nights, the sun began to shine, and Jesus looked out the window. He saw the star of Bethlehem rising in the east..."

Gladys had heard enough. She went in search of Mrs. Lawson, finding her in her bedroom. Gladys knocked on the side of the open door. "May I come in?" she asked.

"Certainly," replied Mrs. Lawson. "What is it?"

Gladys shook her head. "Perhaps I don't under-stand enough of the Yangcheng dialect, but I thought I just heard Yang tell a story about Jesus being on Noah's ark."

Mrs. Lawson looked weary. "I'm sure you heard it correctly," she sighed. "Last week Yang told the muleteers all about Saint Paul parting the Red Sea. The muleteers are begging for Bible stories, and if I'm not there every minute of every night, Yang can't resist stepping in and telling his own versions of the stories for me."

Gladys nodded. Ever since Yang had become a Christian a month before, he'd been eager to share his new faith with the muleteers.

"Still, we mustn't complain," Mrs. Lawson added with surprising optimism. "Yang is doing his best, and the inn is going much better than I ever thought it would."

Gladys nodded again. It had been five months since the Inn of Eight Happinesses had opened. At first she'd had to drag each mule train into the courtyard, but now the new innkeepers had made friends with many of the muleteers, and most nights at the inn the k'ang overflowed with sleep-ing bodies, sometimes up to fifty or more!

Gladys wished she could speak better Chinese. If she could speak the language better, she could help Mrs. Lawson by telling the Bible stories her-self. She decided to spend an extra hour each night learning to tell Bible stories in the Yangcheng dialect. Within a few weeks, Gladys thought, she would know enough to start telling some simple stories. But Gladys didn't have a few weeks. She didn't even have one week in which to learn the Yangcheng dialect better.

Three nights later, as Gladys sat on a soapbox in her room learning some new Chinese words from her notebook, Mrs. Lawson came in and told her it was time for their walk together. Gladys had been behind in her schedule all day. The millet merchant had wanted to talk about the gospel, the woman next door was sick, and Gladys had visited her. She had also spent longer than intended writing a letter to her parents in London. As a result, Gladys had decided to not go on their usual walk that night. Very politely she told Mrs. Lawson she couldn't take a walk with her because she needed to spend more time concentrating on language study.

Mrs. Lawson was gruff, and she could get into a bad temper and say things she didn't mean, but Gladys had never seen her in such a temper as the one she worked herself into over Gladys's not taking a walk with her. Mrs. Lawson told Gladys that if she didn't want to go for a walk with her, then she might as well pack up her bags and leave. When Gladys didn't say anything, Mrs. Lawson got even angrier. She started throwing Gladys's belongings out into the courtyard. An audience quickly gathered at the gate to see what all the commotion was about, and Gladys fled into the kitchen and hid behind a table with Yang. Both of them were shocked by Mrs. Lawson's behavior.

Yang spoke first. "She is old," he said in a soothing voice. "She needs some time to calm down. Why don't you take a little trip to Tsechow and visit the nice lady there. Mrs. Lawson will call for you in a few days when she gets over this."

Gladys closed her eyes and tried to think. By now Mrs. Lawson had finished yelling and slamming the new doors. Finally, there was silence in the house again.

"But I can't walk the trail to Tsechow. It takes two days," said Gladys.

"You will not have to walk. I will arrange for you to go with a mule train," replied Yang.

The journey back through Chowtsun to Tsechow was a sad one for Gladys. Only ten months before, she had set off to find Mrs. Lawson with the highest of hopes, and now she was returning an outcast. Perhaps the director at the China Inland Mission Training School in London had been right after all. Perhaps she really didn't have what it took to be a missionary, thought Gladys.

Gladys had no way of letting Mrs. Smith know she was coming to stay. The mule train was the fastest way to get a message from one place to another, and Gladys was on the first mule train out of Yangcheng following Mrs. Lawson's explosive outburst. Gladys didn't know how she would explain the situation to Mrs. Smith when she got to Tsechow. As it turned out, she didn't need to. Mrs. Smith understood perfectly.

"We all know Mrs. Lawson," she told Gladys when they met. "Her heart is in the right place, but her temper does get in the way sometimes. Over the next few days, she'll think about what she said to you and be sorry. I'm sure a messenger will be at the door in a week or so with a note asking you to come back. She can't do without you, you know." Mrs. Smith held Gladys's hand as she spoke.

Gladys smiled. Hearing what Mrs. Smith had to say made her feel much better.

"You just rest here with us, and you'll hear from Mrs. Lawson in no time," reassured Mrs. Smith, patting the back of Gladys's hand.

Six days later, a messenger came to the door, just as Mrs. Smith had predicted. But he didn't come to deliver the message they'd expected. The messenger talked to Mrs. Smith in the Tsechow dialect. Gladys couldn't understand much of what they said, so she waited for the conversation to end. Finally, after a lot of questions, Mrs. Smith thanked the messenger, bowed to him, and closed the door. With the color draining from her face, she turned to Gladys.

"What is it?" asked Gladys.

"I'm not sure," said Mrs. Smith, frowning. "It's a bit hard to work out really. The messenger was from the mandarin of Tsechow."

Gladys gasped. She knew a mandarin, a Chinese official, didn't trouble himself with small matters.

"It seems Mrs. Lawson has been in some kind of accident," said Mrs. Smith.

"Is she all right?" Gladys interrupted, her heart pounding.

"Well, it's a bit hard to say. The mandarin heard the story after it had been sent through several mule trains. He didn't know where Mrs. Lawson was, but he said she was dying." Mrs. Smith's voice trailed off.

"Dying?" repeated Gladys.

"Yes, but that could mean anything. She may only have a scratch or two. You know how rumors are," said Mrs. Smith, trying to sound reassuring.

Gladys nodded. Her thoughts were whirling. There was only one thing to do.

"I must find her quickly. She needs me," Gladys told Mrs. Smith. "I'll leave at once. Poor Yang, he has so much to do already. I need to help him with Mrs. Lawson."

Mrs. Smith helped Gladys gather supplies for the return journey, and together they found a mule train that would take her back to Yangcheng. Once again Gladys was hoisted onto a mule litter and found herself swaying and bobbing her way back up into the mountains. Every time they passed a mule train going the other way, she would call out and ask if they had any news of the old white devil. No one had any news.

That night, as they entered the village of Chowtsun, Gladys had better luck. An old muleteer who had stayed at the Inn of Eight Happinesses the night before told her that Mrs. Lawson was not in Yangcheng. Yang had told him she'd taken a trip farther up into the mountains. No one knew for sure where she was headed. Yang, apparently, had heard nothing about any accident.

Gladys could feel her stomach churn. Mrs. Lawson wasn't with gentle old Yang after all. She was in the hands of strangers in some mountain village, that is, if she was still alive. Gladys had to find her, and fast.

It took four more days of questions before Gladys found the small, walled village of Chin Shui, where she found Mrs. Lawson. The situation was worse than anything Gladys could have imagined. Gladys found Mrs. Lawson, battered and bruised and covered in dried blood, lying in an open courtyard on a pile of coal. At first Gladys thought Mrs. Lawson was dead. But as she rushed to her, Mrs. Lawson opened her eyes and smiled. "Gladys? Is that you, Gladys? I'm so glad you are here," she said.

Gladys sat down on the heap of coal beside Mrs. Lawson and lifted her friend's head onto her lap. Mrs. Lawson winced in pain. Gladys called for hot water and a cloth and began sponging the black dust and encrusted blood from the old woman's face. As she cleansed Mrs. Lawson, Gladys became more and more angry. She looked up, and above Mrs. Lawson was a balcony with a broken railing. Suddenly, Gladys knew what had happened. Mrs. Lawson had fallen from the balcony, and she had been lying out in the cold on this pile of coal for over a week. No one had tried to move her inside or dress her wounds. Gladys knew that it was only because Mrs. Lawson was such a stubborn old thing that she was still alive.

Gladys took charge. A curious crowd of onlookers had gathered to see what was happening. In her best Yangcheng Chinese, she began to bark out orders.

"You six, over here. We need to lift this woman."

"Bring your lanterns over here."

"Get me some strips of cloth."

"Tell the innkeeper we need a private room with a warm k'ang, and we need it right away."

Just as Gladys had hoped, the unusual experience of being told what to do by a foreign devil spurred them into action. Within an hour, Mrs. Lawson was cleaned up, with her wounds dressed. As far as Gladys could tell, the wounds were not life threatening. Mrs. Lawson seemed to have broken most of the bones in both of her hands, and she had cuts and bruises all over, but nothing else seemed to be wrong.

As she lay on a padded bedroll on a k'ang, Mrs. Lawson looked up at Gladys with grateful eyes. "I'm so glad you came," she repeated over and over.

"So am I," replied Gladys, truthfully. She shuddered as she thought about what might have happened if she'd been just a day later.

When Mrs. Lawson slept, Gladys crept from the room to ask some very important questions. She found the innkeeper and fired away. "Why did you leave Mrs. Lawson on the coal pile for over a week?" she asked.

The innkeeper replied, "Everyone was sure the old white devil was going to die at any minute. We asked ourselves, 'Why cause her pain by moving her?'"

"Then why didn't you clean her wounds?" asked Gladys, continuing her questions.

The innkeeper looked a little sheepish. "She is a white devil, no one wanted to touch her...and she never asked for food, so we did not feed her," he added, guessing Gladys's next question.

Gladys shook her head. Sometimes she wondered whether she would ever understand the villagers' reasoning. How could they let a semiconscious woman starve to death in the cold because she didn't ask for food! Frustrated, Gladys gave up on questioning the innkeeper and went back to see how Mrs. Lawson was doing.

By the next morning, Gladys had decided on a plan of action. She would stay at the inn with Mrs. Lawson until she was strong enough to go back to Yangcheng. The nearest European doctor was in Luan, six days away by mule train, and there was no way Mrs. Lawson could make such a journey in her present condition.

For six weeks, Gladys stayed at the inn in Chin Shui nursing Mrs. Lawson. At first she'd had great hope for Mrs. Lawson's recovery. Her wounds began to heal, and her hands were getting stronger. But something was not right. As the rest of her body got stronger, Mrs. Lawson's back got sorer, and her mind became more confused. Things weren't going as Gladys had hoped, and she wasn't sure what to do about it. Finally, she decided that Mrs. Lawson needed to see the doctor, no matter how torturous the journey to get to him might be. With the help of the cook at the inn, Gladys found a muleteer who was prepared to take her and Mrs. Lawson to Luan.

To make the trip as comfortable as possible, Gladys slung a blanket between two mules and had Mrs. Lawson lifted carefully into it. Mrs. Lawson lay between the two mules for six long days. When they got to the hospital, Gladys wondered whether it had been worth the effort and discomfort after all. The English doctor examined Mrs. Lawson and told Gladys she was slowly dying and there was nothing that he or anyone else could do about it.

The next day, Mrs. Lawson begged Gladys to take her home, so Gladys arranged one last journey for the seventy-four-year-old missionary. The two women returned to Yangcheng, where Yang was waiting for them. When he saw Mrs. Lawson's condition, Yang made a special batch of her favorite soup and ordered her coffin. Two weeks later, Mrs. Lawson was buried in the coffin as Gladys and Yang wept. Mrs. Lawson's funeral was the first Christian burial ever held in Yangcheng.

After the funeral, as Gladys sat beside the grave of the woman she'd come halfway around the world to serve, fear crept into her heart. Mrs. Lawson's death had changed everything. Gladys was now the only European in the district. The closest person she could speak to in English was two days away by mule train. Gladys felt more alone than she'd ever felt before, more alone than when she was in the Siberian wilderness walking along the railroad tracks back to Chita. She was deep in the heart of China with no money, no friends, and no missionary organization to back her.

Still, alone as she was, Gladys told herself she had to go on. All around Yangcheng, people needed to hear the gospel message, and she was the only one left to share that message with them.

Chapter 9

The Honorable
Foot Inspector

No one knew why Mrs. Lawson had gone to Chin Shui. Perhaps she was looking for a new location to start another inn. Perhaps she needed to get away and think about things after she'd lost her temper and thrown Gladys out. Whatever the reason, Mrs. Lawson never told anybody why she was leaving Yangcheng or where she was going.

Gladys soon discovered something else Mrs. Lawson hadn't told her: how much it cost to run the inn. It was true that the Inn of Eight Happinesses made enough money to cover the cost of rent, coal for the k'ang, and food, but each year a large amount was paid in taxes to the mandarin. Mrs. Lawson had paid this amount from her small monthly income and had said nothing about it to Gladys or

Yang. But with Mrs. Lawson gone, there was no extra income to pay the taxes, which were now due.

Gladys had no idea where the money to pay these taxes would come from. She discussed the problem with Yang, who offered only one solution: She must go and bow before the mandarin.

"What difference would that make?" Gladys asked impatiently. "I don't see any point to it."

"You don't need to have a point. It is just something you should do. You will see the point when you get there," replied the old cook.

"How do I do it, then? What do I say?" Gladys asked.

Yang frowned. "That's a difficult question. I will ask in town." With that he headed out the door.

Yang was back about an hour later, but he didn't have good news to report. Since Mrs. Lawson and Gladys were the first two foreigners to live in Yangcheng, there were no set rules for how many times Gladys should bow to the mandarin, or exactly what she should say to him, or in what order. This posed a difficult problem because, as Yang pointed out, making a mistake in protocol when addressing the mandarin could be deadly. Gladys thought of the mandarin's soldier with his long curved sword at the execution in the marketplace and shuddered at just how deadly some mistakes can be with the mandarin.

In the end, Yang decided that Gladys should put on her best clothes and ask the mandarin's secretary whether he would grant her an appointment to see the mandarin. If he agreed, they would then work out the details of what she should say at the meeting. Gladys just shook her head. She had no "best" clothes. The only clothes she had were the quilted blue trousers and jacket she was wearing, and they weren't suitable clothes to bow before a mandarin in. The mandarin was the highest official in the district. It would be completely disrespectful to have an audience with him in such clothes, and Gladys didn't have the money to buy any other clothes. The case was closed. Gladys would not be seeing the mandarin anytime soon. She would just have to find some other way to deal with paying the taxes.

About a week later, Gladys was upstairs writing a letter to some friends in England when she heard a commotion downstairs. She could hear unfamiliar sounds, like the clanging of bells and the rhythmic thump of marching feet. She hurried downstairs to see what it was. Yang met her in the doorway. "The mandarin is coming. The mandarin is coming," he blurted out.

Gladys was excited. The mandarin rarely came out of his palace, or "yamen," as it was called. If she hurried, she could see him passing by the Inn of Eight Happinesses!

"Where is the best place to see him pass?" she asked Yang.

Yang stared at her. Then a look of understanding crossed his face. "No, no. He is not passing by, he is coming here. Here to the Inn of Eight Happinesses. He wants to talk to you."

Gladys's eyes grew wider and wider. "But why me?" she asked.

"I don't know," Yang replied. "You should have gone and bowed to him when I told you to. Now maybe he is angry."

Yang backed his way out the door, and before Gladys could ask another question, he had turned and fled down the street in the opposite direction from the mandarin. As she watched him disappear around the corner, Gladys thought he ran surprisingly fast for an old man.

By now the procession was so close that Gladys could see the neat rows of soldiers marching in front of the mandarin's satin-draped sedan chair, which was carried on the shoulders of eight servants. Behind the chair were several advisors dressed in beautiful embroidered gowns.

Gladys stood rooted to the spot, unable to do any more than pull a few wayward strands of hair back into her bun and adjust her well-worn jacket.

Suddenly a shout came from the soldier leading the parade, and the entire procession came to a halt. The servants set the sedan chair down, and with a loud clang of bells, another servant pulled back the curtain around it and offered the mandarin his arm. With a flourish, the mandarin took it and stepped out. His eyes swept the courtyard. Gladys bowed low, and then bowed again. She wished she knew what to do next, but she didn't. So she bowed once again, just in case it was necessary, and then she waited for the mandarin to make the next move.

He broke the silence. "You are Gladys Aylward, I presume?" he asked.

"Yes, sir," Gladys replied, in her best Yangcheng dialect.

"I have come to ask your help," the mandarin continued.

"My help?" Gladys echoed in amazement. She couldn't think of a way she could possibly help a mandarin.

"Yes," replied the mandarin. "I have a problem, and only you can solve it for me. There is a new government in Nanking, as you must know, and as all new governments do, they have made new rules. One of the new rules is that foot binding is to be stopped in China. The new government is holding each mandarin personally responsible to make sure foot binding stops in his district."

Gladys nodded. She was pleased to hear that the cruel practice was going to be banned, but she had no idea how it involved her.

"So," continued the mandarin, looking rather proud of himself, "the government has given me a problem. I need someone to be a foot inspector. A man would not do, because men are not to look at a woman's feet. I need a female foot inspector. But where, I asked myself, would I find a woman who could travel on foot over rough roads and climb mountains to reach the small villages to make sure every girl's feet have been unbound? Only a woman with unbound feet could do that. And I asked myself, in all of China, who is the woman who speaks the Yangcheng dialect and has unbound feet? That woman will be my foot inspector."

The mandarin stopped for a moment to smile at his logic. Then he proceeded. "There is only one such woman in the whole district, and it is you, Gladys Aylward!"

Gladys smiled weakly, trying to grasp what she was hearing. Was the mandarin offering her a job or giving her a command? She wasn't sure.

Before she could decide, the mandarin continued. "Two of my soldiers will go with you, and I will give you a mule to ride. When you speak, people will listen to you as if I myself were speaking. To disobey you is to disobey me." He looked down at his sword, and Gladys knew exactly what he meant.

"I will pay you for your service. Do you have any questions?" the mandarin added.

Gladys knew she had a million questions inside, if she could just think straight for a moment. "But," she finally stammered, "I'm a Christian, not a foot inspector."

As she spoke, a thought flashed through her mind. As a foot inspector, she would get to visit every village and every farm in the district with an escort from the mandarin. Not to mention getting paid for it. She thought of all the Bible stories she could tell along the way. She could use her position to spread the gospel message throughout the entire district. But would the mandarin let her do that? Gladys had to find out.

"Wherever I went on behalf of your excellency," she continued more boldly now, "I would speak of my God and my faith, and I would try to make others believe as I do."

She stood, her heart thumping, waiting for the mandarin's reply. The mandarin stroked his mustache for a few moments. Only the crying of a baby in a distant house broke the silence.

Gladys began to wonder whether she had said something insulting. The mandarin had complete power over the people of Yangcheng and the surrounding district. What if she had offended him with her boldness? Would her head be the next one on the wall?

Finally the mandarin spoke. "It is most important that foot binding stop immediately. As to your religion, it is not of any importance to me. Speak of what you will. If the women become Christians, they will want their daughters to have unbound feet like you, and that will be a good thing."

Gladys bowed gratefully.

"I will send the soldiers and the mule for you in the morning to begin your work. I expect you to report to me regularly on your progress. Come to the yamen, and my secretary will arrange an audience with me."

With that, the mandarin bowed to Gladys, turned, and climbed back into his sedan chair. Gladys bowed deeply and watched the procession move back along the street. As it moved out of sight, Gladys let out a deep sigh of relief. After worrying so hard about money to live on and to keep the inn going, she had her answer, and it was a much better answer than anything she'd been able to come up with on her own.

The next morning, Gladys was up early and waiting in the courtyard for her escorts to arrive with the mule. As she waited, she tried to imagine how she might go about getting mothers and fathers to unbind their daughters' feet. After all, binding the feet of baby girls had been going on in China for countless generations. People probably weren't going to take kindly to being told by a foreign devil to stop the practice. Gladys decided that this could well turn out to be a more challenging task for her than dragging the mules into the courtyard of the Inn of Eight Happinesses as she'd had to in the beginning.

The feet of baby girls were wrapped tight with linen bandages. Since the bones in a baby's feet are soft and pliable, the feet slowly doubled over until the toes and front half of the foot were tucked underneath. By the time a girl was twelve or thirteen years of age, her feet were permanently doubled in half. By then, all a girl could do on them was hobble around slowly. Girls couldn't run or play like the boys did. But the new Nationalist government had sensibly decided that the practice needed to end. It outlawed the binding of the feet of girls under age ten. That way, a whole generation of girls would grow up without bound feet, and the men, who had been taught that bound feet were desirable, would have no choice but to marry girls with "big" feet.

Gladys heard the clip-clop of a mule's hooves on cobblestones, and soon the mule and two soldiers were standing in the courtyard. The soldiers bowed to Gladys, and with a flourish, one of them lifted her onto the mule litter, and they were on their way over the barren mountains.

The first village Gladys came to was located on the side of a steep river gorge. The cramped houses were made of mud and had green tiled roofs. News traveled around the village fast, and within a few minutes of entering the gate, the village elder was bowing to Gladys. The soldiers told the elder why they had come to his village, and the elder called the village together in the marketplace. Soon women with baskets of laundry, men with hoes, and little children with runny noses were all assembled.

The elder introduced Gladys. "This is the honorable foot inspector for the mandarin," he began. "She is here to inspect the feet of every girl in the village. She has orders to see that every girl under age ten has her feet unbound, and she will come back to see they stay that way."

A shocked silence came over the crowd.

"Furthermore," the elder added, "if this new law is not carried out, the father involved will be sent to prison. The foot inspector is to be obeyed."

Finally, there was a gasp from the audience, followed by a rumble of complaints, not loud enough for the elder to identify individuals but loud enough to frighten Gladys. Despite what the elder had just said, Gladys had doubts about how she was going to get the people to obey her.

Gladys decided she needed to do something impressive to get everyone's attention, so she gestured for the soldiers to follow her. She walked boldly over to the nearest house. Through the open door she saw a little girl of about three sitting on the k'ang. As Gladys walked in, a woman scooped up the little girl and held her on her knee. Two other women appeared at the doorway to watch.

"Unbind that girl's feet immediately," commanded Gladys in her most official-sounding voice.

The woman began to unwrap the linen bandages. Soon the little girl's feet were free. Even at three years of age, the girl's toes were folded over, and her feet were white from a lack of blood reaching them. Gladys had never actually seen bound feet without their linen wrap before. The sight of the little girl's feet made her feel sick to her stomach. She knelt in front of the girl and began to massage her feet. Slowly a pink color began to return to them, and the girl's toes began to uncurl into their proper position.

"See these little feet. God made this little girl's feet just like a little boy's feet." Gladys glanced around to make sure the soldiers were still outside before she continued. "If I come back and find that anyone has bound this girl's feet again, that person will be put in prison."

Gladys stood and walked out the door. She entered the next house, and the house after that, and repeated the procedure. By mid-afternoon, she was satisfied that the feet of all the young girls in the village had been unbound. The elder invited her to spend the night at his house, and so Gladys spent a pleasant evening telling him stories from the Bible.

The next morning, Gladys and the soldiers were off to the next village, keeping a watchful eye out as they looked for families living in the caves dotted throughout the mountains. At the next village, the same scene repeated itself, only this time, Gladys was feeling a little braver. Wherever she went, she was respected and obeyed.

It took Gladys several months to visit every village and every family in the district. After she had been through the district once, she reported to the mandarin that there were no more young girls with bound feet in his domain. However, the mandarin was a cautious man, and he insisted Gladys continue her rounds of the district, checking up on everyone. This suited Gladys just fine, because she'd discovered that once a little girl's feet were unbound and she was able to walk around normally, most parents wondered why they had ever bound them in the first place. They agreed that it was a silly custom, and they were glad to be rid of it. Big feet, they decided were useful, not ugly. This change of heart meant that Gladys had nothing to do but travel around with an escort of soldiers and tell Bible stories. It wasn't long before the villagers all looked forward with great delight to the foot inspector's visit.

The year rolled by. When Gladys was away on her trips, Yang looked after things at the inn. And with no Mrs. Lawson around to talk to in English, Gladys was soon fluent in the Yangcheng dialect. In fact, she spoke it better than many of the locals did. And her storytelling was producing results. Soon small bands of Christians began to form in the villages she visited.

Things couldn't have worked out better for Gladys. She visited the mandarin regularly, and he seemed to be impressed with the job she had done. As it turned out, he was so impressed that when he needed the services of the bravest person in Yangcheng, he summoned Gladys.

Chapter 10

Ai-weh-deh

Running the Inn of Eight Happinesses kept Yang very busy when Gladys was away on her foot-inspection trips. It was a great relief to them both when Mrs. Smith in Tsechow sent Lu Yung-cheng, a new convert, to help with the work at the inn. Mrs. Smith even paid Lu's monthly salary so that he was not a financial burden on Gladys. Lu Yung-cheng was a good worker, and Gladys enjoyed having the extra pair of hands around to help with the work. She enjoyed Lu's company, too, and was relieved to have someone around who could make sure Yang's stories in the evenings came out the way they were recorded in the Bible.

Several days after returning from a foot-inspection trip to some of the villages west of Yangcheng,

119

Gladys stood in the kitchen stirring a pot of soup. Lu Yung-cheng was also in the kitchen preparing vegetables. They were busy talking about how things were going around the inn, when they heard a commotion in the courtyard. Suddenly, a messenger from the mandarin burst into the house. He waved a piece of red paper and began talking. He spoke so fast that no one could understand what he was saying, so Gladys had him slow down and repeat himself. It seemed there was a riot going on at the prison, and the prisoners were killing each other. As a result, the mandarin had summoned Gladys to the prison.

Gladys shook her head. "That's crazy. I've never been near the prison in my life. There's nothing I could do there. You must have the wrong house."

"But he has an official summons," said Lu, pointing at the red paper the messenger was holding.

The messenger waved the paper at Gladys. Lu Yung-cheng reached out, took the paper, and looked at it. "It definitely says the mandarin has sent for you," he confirmed.

Gladys couldn't believe what she was hearing. She was the official foot inspector. What could foot inspection possibly have to do with a prison riot?

"You go," she urged Lu Yung-cheng. "There must be a mistake. You can straighten it out. The prison is a place for men, not for a woman."

Lu shook his head. "You have to go. You have been summoned. If you don't go, you'll end up in prison for disobeying an official summons."

Gladys sighed. She was still weary from all her traveling, and the last thing she wanted to do was go near the prison. Still, she reached for her jacket and hurriedly followed the messenger to the eastern wall of town where the prison was located. As she got closer to the prison, bloodcurdling screams and cries for help grew louder and louder. The messenger led Gladys through the crowd that had gathered outside the prison and into the prison office located on the outer wall of the prison. Inside, standing with six soldiers, was the governor of the prison. A look of relief came over his face when he saw Gladys.

"I've been waiting for you," he began, as he bowed to her. "The convicts are killing each other, and my soldiers are too frightened to go back inside."

Gladys nodded weakly. "I am very sorry to hear that, but I am a foot inspector. What does this have to do with me?"

"You must go in and stop the fighting," replied the governor firmly.

Gladys felt herself getting dizzy. "I must go in there and stop them?" she echoed numbly, thinking of the murderers and robbers inside. "But I'm only a woman. I don't know anything about fighting. If I go in there they'll kill me."

The governor smiled in triumph. "No they won't. You are always telling everyone that you have the living God in you, so how could they kill you?" he reasoned.

Feeling faint, Gladys reached for the wall to steady herself. "You want me to step into a prison riot because I have the living God in me and you think I can't be killed?" she gasped.

Her mind whirled. How could she explain to the prison governor it wasn't that simple. Christians could be killed like anyone else, and Gladys was pretty sure if she went into the prison, that's what was going to happen to her. The eyes of the governor and all of the soldiers were on her, waiting to see what she would do.

When Gladys said nothing, the governor repeated himself. "You and the living God can go in there together and get the men to stop fighting. Otherwise, none of them will be left alive."

Gladys had an important decision to make. If she refused to help, word would quickly travel around Yangcheng and throughout the surrounding villages that there was no living God in Gladys. But if she went into the prison? Gladys didn't even dare think about what might happen to her. But when she thought about the people of Yangcheng and the surrounding villages, she could make only one decision. Gladys turned to the prison governor and said, "I will go in."

Before Gladys had time to think about what she'd just said, a soldier turned the key in the lock of the huge iron gate that guarded the entrance to the prison. As soon as the gate was open wide enough, the governor pushed Gladys inside. "God, protect me now, and give me strength to do this,"

Gladys quickly prayed as the iron gate clanged shut behind her.

In front of her was a pitch-black tunnel about twenty yards long. The tunnel opened out into the prison courtyard at the opposite end. Gladys stood paralyzed with fear for a moment, afraid to go forward and unable to go back. Then slowly she began feeling her way forward through the tunnel towards the screams at the end of it. A few moments later, she was standing in bright sunlight, looking out at a more horrible scene than the one she'd viewed at the execution in the marketplace. Blood was splattered everywhere. Men lay dead or dying all around. Gladys watched in horror as a prisoner with a huge machete lunged at a group of men crouched in a corner. The men scattered, climbing over dead bodies to escape. One of the men ran in Gladys's direction. The prisoner with the machete raced after him. The fleeing man hid behind a box, but the machete-wielding man saw him. Gladys watched in terror as the machete was drawn into the air over the fleeing man's head.

Without thinking, Gladys stepped out of the shadows and bravely yelled, "Stop at once, and give me that machete."

The prisoner turned in Gladys's direction, his black eyes gleaming with evil. When he saw Gladys, he stopped and held the machete motionless in midair. Then, as if some outside force were controlling him, he let the machete go, and it clattered loudly to the ground. The noise startled everyone in the prison courtyard. All eyes were now fixed on Gladys, who knew she had only a few seconds to gain control.

"All of you," she commanded, "drop your weapons and come over here." She pointed in front of her. "Get into a line now." As she said this, she thought frantically of what to say next. She was an unarmed woman alone in a prison filled with desperate men. If she said the wrong thing, the favor she seemed to have with the men at that moment would be lost, and anything could happen.

The men began to line up in front of her. Gladys looked at them. She'd never seen men in such a sad state. They were desperately thin. They had open, oozing sores all over their bodies and so many lice that Gladys could see them weaving in and out of their hair. No wonder the men had rioted. They had been stripped of all their human dignity. In an instant, Gladys knew what she would say next.

She cleared her throat. "I have been sent in here to find out what the problem is and to help solve it," she began. "But I do not think I can talk to the governor on your behalf until you clean up some of this mess."

She swept her hand in the direction of the courtyard. Somehow she knew it was important to get the prisoners to work together, and quickly. "Clean up this mess, and then we will talk about what I should tell the governor for you."

Obediently, the men began to sweep up the courtyard. One prisoner brought a machete and several knives to Gladys. Others began to move the dead bodies into a pile. One of the men came over to talk to Gladys. He introduced himself as Feng and apologized for the riot on behalf of all the prisoners.

"I don't know what happened," Feng said, shaking his head. "Somehow it all became too much, and someone started a fight. We really didn't mean to kill anybody."

Something about Feng's manner caused Gladys to trust him. "What were you all doing when the riot broke out?" she asked.

"Doing?" asked Feng. "We were doing the same thing we do every day—sitting and waiting for the day to end."

"But don't you have jobs in here? Things to keep you busy?" asked Gladys.

Feng shook his head. "No, we sit and wait all day. Some of the men starve to death because they have no relatives to bring them food, and others die because there's no reason to live. I was a Buddhist priest before I was accused of stealing and sentenced here for eight years. I doubt that I shall ever get out. The cold kills many in here."

Gladys glanced down at the thin rags Feng was wearing. Her body shivered unconsciously as she envisioned how cold the men must get in such clothes, especially in the dead of winter. Just as Gladys was about to reply to Feng, the prison governor walked up behind her. He bowed to her. "Thank you very much," he began. "You have done a great service to our town. I will take over now."

The governor took the machete and knives from Gladys's hand. Gladys turned to walk back through the tunnel towards the iron gate, when she felt an irresistible urge to do something that took as much bravery as walking into the riot in the first place. She turned back to the governor. "This cannot go on," she said in a loud voice.

The governor looked stunned. "What do you mean?" he asked.

Gladys pointed at the rags Feng was wearing. "It is no wonder these men rioted. You or I would have, too. Look how thin these men are. Some of them are starving, and they have nothing to do day after day!"

"Nothing to do?" asked the governor. "I don't understand. They are in prison. Of course they do nothing."

"But they should do something," said Gladys, pressing the point. "All men need something to do. Get them looms and let them weave themselves some clothes. Let them grow some vegetables to eat. These men need something to do."

Gladys searched the governor's face for some sign of what he was thinking. Finally, the governor spoke. "You have given me much to think about. We will talk about this again later."

Gladys thought of one more thing before she left. Boldly she said, "I have promised the men you will not punish them for this. They have promised not to riot again."

The prison governor nodded. "As you wish," he

said. "It is amazing you got them to stop, whatever you promised them."

Gladys smiled and turned to Feng. "I will be back to visit you, and I will see what I can do for all of you."

Feng bowed deeply. "Thank you, *Ai-weh-deh*," he replied.

It was several days before Gladys learned that the word *Ai-weh-deh* meant "virtuous one." Only then did she understand that Feng, a Buddhist priest, had paid her, a Christian, a great compliment.

Gladys was true to her word. She began to visit the prisoners every day. She read them stories from the Bible and taught them about basic hygiene. She also visited the prison governor every day until he agreed to make some changes in the way the prison was run. Since there was no money for "extras," Gladys came up with her own ways of making the prisoners' lives more useful. Some friends of the governor agreed to donate two old looms to the prison, and Gladys begged yarn from the local merchants. She also begged a miller's wheel so that the prisoners could grind their own grain. Gladys even taught the men how to breed rabbits for sale. Within a few months of the riot, the prisoners were all warmly dressed and eating well. Gladys had kept her end of the bargain.

News of the changes in the prison spread throughout the district. Soon everyone was calling Gladys Ai-weh-deh. Gladys Aylward, the housemaid from London, who, when she arrived three years before had been viewed as nothing more than a foreign devil, had won a place in the hearts of the people of Yangcheng, first as the foot inspector, and now as a riot stopper and prison reformer. What would be next?

Chapter 11

Vehicles That Flew
Like Insects

Gladys hurried along the narrow street past the coal merchant and the candle seller. She was on her way to the yamen to report to the mandarin. She visited him every time she came back from one of her foot-inspection tours. Lately her reports had all been the same: No more girls with bound feet were to be found in the district. The practice had been done away with.

Gladys was thinking of how to make her report interesting, when she noticed an old woman she'd never seen before sitting at the edge of the street. Gladys looked at her closely. The old woman was wearing heavy silver jewelry and jade hairpins, all of which were quite usual in Yangcheng. But her bright green cloth shoes really caught Gladys's attention. Gladys had never seen anyone in Shansi province with shoes that color. It simply wasn't a color that was used for shoes.

Curiosity got the better of her, and Gladys decided to find out a little more about the woman. She walked over to her. Just as she was about to say something, a tiny, scraggly child peered around from behind the woman. Gladys was horrified by the child's condition. The child was dirty and dressed in rags, and her stomach poked out like that of a starving child. The little girl shielded her eyes from the sunlight and looked up at Gladys.

"This child is very sick," Gladys said to the woman.

"That's none of your business," replied the old woman with a strange accent. "Besides, if she dies I can get another one to replace her anytime I want."

"You're mistaken," said Gladys. "It is my business. I am Ai-weh-deh, and I am on my way to see the mandarin himself. You had better do something with that girl. Now!" She put as much authority into her voice as possible.

"Don't want her, don't need her," said the woman in a singsong voice. "Give me two dollars and she's yours."

Gladys recoiled in horror.

The woman watched her shrewdly. "All right, you drive a hard bargain. A dollar and a half." The woman delivered a smile that revealed an almost toothless mouth.

Gladys was upset and angry. This stranger with green shoes was treating the little girl as if she were a goat or a chicken being bought for a feast.

"I don't buy children. I'm going to talk to the mandarin about you," Gladys said. And with that, she walked off towards the yamen.

An hour and a half later, after going through all the formalities of greeting the mandarin and telling him about the child seller only a hundred yards from the yamen, Gladys asked him directly, "What do we do about it?"

The mandarin's eyes fixed on Gladys, and with great emphasis he said, "We do not do anything. I agree it is not good that there are child sellers, but there is nothing we can do about it. The sellers belong to powerful groups of criminals. If we attempt to stop them or interfere in any way, they will make us very sorry."

After he had spoken, the mandarin picked up his hammer and struck the gong beside his chair, signaling that the audience was over and that Gladys had been dismissed. As Gladys walked towards the door, the mandarin gave a command. "Under no circumstances are you to go near the child seller again. Nor are you to repeat the conversation we had about it with anybody. That is an order!"

Gladys's heart beat heavily in her chest. Mandarin or not, she knew she had to speak her mind. She turned to face him, bowed slightly again, and said, "I came to China because God sent me. I did not come to obey your laws if they are different from the laws of my God. I will ask God what I should do about the child seller, and I will do as He says, not as you or anyone else tells me."

The mandarin's mouth dropped open. Gladys supposed it was the first time anyone had ever spoken to him like that, and certainly the first time a woman had, and a foreign woman at that. She did not wait for his reaction. She bowed one last time, turned quickly, and walked away.

Gladys was still trying to decide what to do about the situation, when she turned into the street where she had seen the child seller. Sure enough, the woman was still there. As soon as the woman spotted Gladys, she yelled, "Lady, I give you best bargain. Only one hundred and fifty *cash*."

"I don't have one hundred and fifty *cash*, and besides I don't want the child," Gladys shot back.

Even as these words came out of her mouth, Gladys realized she could not leave the little girl to possibly die in the hands of such a heartless person. She stopped and turned and stared at the woman. "I do not have that much *cash*, but I will give you what I have in my pocket."

The woman smiled slyly. "And how much would that be?" she asked.

Gladys fished around in her jacket pocket and pulled out a few copper *cash* coins, equal to ninepence in English money. She held the coins out on her open palm for the woman to see.

"Done," the woman declared, grasping for the money. "Take her away."

Gladys took the hand of the little girl, who she decided must be about four or five years old. Together they continued on down the street. By the time Gladys reached the inn, the enormity of what she had just done began to dawn on her. She had just bought, or adopted, as she preferred to think of it, a little girl. Just like that, she had become a mother.

Ninepence, as the girl quickly became known, gulped down every scrap of food she was given. Within weeks she had turned into a healthy, happy little girl. She loved living at the inn, and Gladys never had a moment of regret that she'd followed her heart and not the mandarin's command.

One day, after Ninepence had been living at the inn about six months, Gladys was standing on the upstairs balcony. Suddenly, she saw Ninepence come running through the gate into the courtyard.

"Ai-weh-deh," Ninepence yelled, "are you very hungry tonight?"

Gladys thought the question rather odd, but she answered it. "Yes, I am, and Yang is making us a delicious millet stew."

Ninepence looked up at her. "I'm going to eat a little less for dinner. If I eat a little less, would you eat a little less, too?" she asked.

"Why would we do that?" inquired Gladys.

"I found a boy out here, and he is hungry," Ninepence said, pointing to the gate. "If I eat less, and you eat less, and we put those two lesses together, we would have enough to feed him, too."

Gladys smiled to herself. Ninepence was always on the lookout for children in need. "Yes, I will eat less with you, and the boy can eat with us. Bring him in," she said.

And so it was, that an eight-year-old orphan boy also became part of the family. Gladys named him Less, in honor of their first meal together.

Now that Gladys had two "adopted" children, she felt she should become a Chinese citizen so that no matter what happened, she would not have to be separated from them. She talked to the mandarin about this matter, and even though she had taken Ninepence against his instructions, he agreed to help her. Together they filled out many papers, and in 1936, Gladys Aylward became the first foreign missionary ever to become a Chinese citizen.

About the same time, Mrs. Smith, her dear friend in Tsechow, died. Throughout the six years Gladys had been in Yangcheng, Mrs. Smith had encouraged and supported her. She had been kind and understanding, not to mention the nearest person Gladys could have a conversation with in English after Mrs. Lawson died. Soon after, a Welsh couple, Jean and David Davies, came to Tsechow to take Mrs. Smith's place. The Davieses were an easy-going couple, and Gladys enjoyed their company, though she sometimes had to be reminded to speak to them in English because she'd become so used to speaking in the Yangcheng dialect.

Life settled into a happy pattern for Gladys. A local convert who was a widow came to live at the inn to take care of the children when Gladys made her foot-inspection tours. Almost every village that Gladys visited now had a small church. Often when she was walking through the fields, Gladys would hear the sound of Christian hymns ringing through the valleys. The local people loved to sing them as they worked.

Gladys had made many friends among the muleteers, and every night the Inn of Eight Happinesses was filled to overflowing with them. Gladys's family was growing, too. Ninepence had found a toddler wandering alone on a hillside outside the city wall and had brought him home with her. Although Gladys had sent the town crier out day after day to find who the boy belonged to, no one ever claimed him. So Boa-Boa became Gladys's third child.

That same year, the Yellow River, which borders Shansi province to the south and west, flooded. Many refugees fled to higher ground in the mountains. One of them was a small boy named Francis, who had no one to take care of him, and Gladys took him into her growing family. The mandarin gave Gladys her next child. He and Gladys had become good friends, and he trusted her judgment completely. He had responsibility for an eight-year-old orphan girl, and he decided that Gladys was the best person to look after her. The girl's name was Lan Hsiang, and she joined Ninepence, Less, Boa-Boa, and Francis at the Inn of Eight Happinesses.

Of course, Gladys had plenty to keep her busy with five children to look after. But as each year went by, the people of Yangcheng district and the mandarin began to rely on her more and more to help solve their problems. When the mandarin had an important decision to make, he would seek Gladys for suggestions. When the prison governor wanted his children to go to school, he asked Gladys to start one, which she did. But there was one problem Gladys could not have solved, even if she'd known it was coming. At first it didn't seem like anything unusual. The muleteers brought vague news about war. No one thought much of it, because China had been at war with parts of itself or its neighbors for centuries. Gladys remembered not being able to get past Chita on the train because of an unofficial war between China and Russia.

As time passed, however, this war began to sound different from other local wars. It wasn't just another border war. The Japanese had actually invaded Manchuria and set up their own government there. And they didn't seem satisfied with just occupying Manchuria. Japanese troops were now moving into more of northeastern China. Still, it all seemed such a long way away from Yangcheng, nestled among the arid peaks and valleys of southern Shansi province.

Then one clear spring morning in 1938, the citizens of Yangcheng heard a strange buzzing sound in the air. They rushed from their houses and into the streets to see what could be making the sound.

They scanned the skies. Soon their efforts were rewarded by the shapes of five airplanes glistening silver in the morning sun. A bright red dot on a white square decorated the airplanes' wings. The townspeople cheered and applauded. None of them had ever seen an airplane before, though many had heard that there were vehicles that flew like insects. As the people watched, hatches on the underside of the planes opened, and what looked to the people like black boxes fell out. The townspeople cheered and applauded some more. Small children were swung up onto their parents' shoulders for a better look, and the entire yamen guard was given permission to run outdoors to see the magnificent sight. Then the first "black box" hit the ground, producing a loud explosion.

"Bombs," someone yelled. "Get inside. They're bombs."

Hardly anyone knew what a bomb was, but people could see for themselves what a bomb did. The citizens of Yangcheng screamed and dove for cover. Throughout the city, bombs fell, making huge, gaping holes where there had been buildings and leaving people dead in the streets who moments before had thrilled to see their first airplane.

Gladys was upstairs in the inn praying with some new converts when the attack occurred. She'd heard the planes at the last moment, and before she could react, a bomb had landed on the southeast corner of the inn. Gladys heard the deafening noise, the inn shuddered, and the floor on which she was standing gave way. Gladys crashed down to the floor below and lost consciousness. When she came to a short time later, her body was pinned under a crushing weight of bricks and beams. She could hear voices amid the sounds of destruction. She yelled for help. An hour later, the last pieces of timber were lifted off her legs, and she was free. She stood up gingerly; her body was cut and bruised, but she had no broken bones.

After a quick drink of water, Gladys set to work helping to free others who had been upstairs praying with her and were now trapped in the rubble. By lunchtime, they'd all been found and pulled out alive. But on the street outside the inn, another bomb had killed nine villagers.

It was nearly impossible for Gladys and the other townspeople to believe what had happened to them that bright spring morning. A normal morning had turned into a nightmare in the course of a few seconds. No one had had the slightest idea that the Japanese would bomb the village. In an instant, the townspeople's lives had been turned upside down.

Gladys picked her way through what was left of the Inn of Eight Happinesses looking for her first-aid kit. As she searched, her children, who'd been in school when the attack occurred, came running through the gate. Gladys swept them into her arms and kissed them, thankful that they were all safe. She fought back sobs as she imagined what it would have been like if even one of them had been killed. When they had finished hugging, Gladys told the children to stay near the inn and begin clearing away the rubble while she went into town to see what she could do to help.

Minutes later, gripping her first-aid kit, Gladys turned the corner at the end of the street. The town was devastated. Streets had enormous craters in them. Where there had been shops and houses piles of rubble were smoldering. But it was the sight of the people—bleeding people, screaming people, dead people—that made Gladys stop in her tracks. Gladys looked down at her puny first-aid kit and for a moment considered turning back. She saw so much destruction, and she had so little to work with. Then she heard a groan nearby. She looked around and saw a woman's head poking out from a pile of bricks. The sight of the woman spurred Gladys into action. Gladys looked around again. People who didn't seem to be hurt were wandering around in a daze. Gladys recognized the vegetable seller and one of the schoolteachers.

"People," she yelled. "Everyone over here at once."

Slowly, as if in a trance, people began to gather around Gladys. "We must work together. There is a lot to do. We will start here," she said, pointing to the spot where the groaning woman's head was protruding from the pile of bricks.

"The injured people must be taken to the yamen. The dead bodies must be dragged out the

west gate and buried in one big plot in the cemetery. And we must clear a path through the main
street." Gladys sounded a lot more confident than
she felt. To her surprise, though, people began doing
as she said.

Gladys worked all afternoon and through the
night, bandaging wounds and crudely setting broken bones. As the first hint of dawn touched the
horizon, she looked up to see the mandarin looming over her. How strange it was to see him walking
alone without his sedan chair and servants. He
bowed to Gladys, who bowed back. The simple act
of bowing to her friend soothed her nerves.

The mandarin had been looking for Gladys. He
had news, and it was not good. A messenger from
the mandarin of Luan had just reached Yangcheng
to warn the people that the Japanese had captured
Luan and were now marching towards Tsechow.
From there it was only a two days' march to
Yangcheng.

With chilling clarity, Gladys understood why the
Japanese had bombed Yangcheng. They were weak-
ening the town so that when they invaded in a few
days, it could be easily overrun. The destruction
that lay around them was not the end of their suf-
fering; it was only the beginning.

Chapter 12

All That You Are
and All That You Do

Soon everyone in Yangcheng understood that it was only a matter of time before the Japanese army arrived. After seeing the death and destruction the air raid had caused, nobody wanted to be around when the troops marched in. The mandarin, Gladys, the prison governor, and an important merchant formed a relief committee. Together they made decisions that would affect everyone in Yangcheng.

The committee's first decision was that as soon as the dead had been buried, everyone should leave Yangcheng. If the citizens scattered among relatives and friends on the farms and in the tiny villages dotted over the mountains, they would have less chance of being caught by the enemy. This also

141

meant that Yangcheng would be a ghost town when the Japanese arrived. Most of the buildings in the town were damaged or destroyed, and the committee hoped that if the people took their livestock and food supplies with them, the Japanese would have no reason to stay. Perhaps the soldiers would march right through Yangcheng so that later on the townspeople could return in safety.

Everyone found somewhere to go. The prison governor chained the prisoners together and marched them off to nearby farmhouses. The mandarin chose to take his wives and children to a small village in the foothills. Yang returned to his family in the countryside. And Gladys, who was now responsible for a band of about forty people that included her children, orphans from the attack on Yangcheng, and new converts, went to the settlement of Bei Chai Chuang. Gladys knew the district better than any other person in all Shansi. She had crisscrossed the region many times looking for girls with bound feet who might be tucked away on farms in the smallest of valleys or in houses perched on the sides of mountains.

Because of her travels, Gladys knew that Bei Chai Chuang was the perfect place for them all to go. Physically it was well suited. Gladys doubted that the Japanese would ever find the place. It wasn't on any map, and there were no roads to it, just a steep climb over rocky outcrops. The whole community consisted of only eight houses enclosed by a wall, but the houses weren't where Gladys intended to stay. In the surrounding hills were several large caves, where the local herdsmen housed their goats, pigs, and sheep during the winter. The caves were warm and dry, but more importantly, they were almost impossible to spot from the outside. Not only were they a perfect hiding place, but Gladys had many friends among the people of Bei Chai Chuang. She knew she could count on them to share their food and show them kindness.

With a heavy heart, Gladys led the group out of Yangcheng. As she walked through the west gate, she looked back one last time at the fairy-tale city she called home. How different it looked now than when she'd first laid eyes on it from a mule train eight years before. No longer were brightly colored banners waving in the breeze, the beautiful curved roofs were destroyed, and thin spirals of smoke still drifted upwards from the ruins. The smell of plum blossoms filled the air, and Gladys wondered whether anyone would ever come back to Yangcheng to pick the plums. Tears slid down her cheeks as she reached for Boa-Boa's hand and began the trek from Yangcheng to the caves of Bei Chai Chuang.

It took nearly a whole day for the weary group to reach their destination. The people of Bei Chai Chuang welcomed them warmly, and soon the caves were swept and made ready for the guests. That night, as they sat around a campfire inside the cave, Gladys and some of the others told the people of Bei Chai Chuang the terrible story of the attack on Yangcheng. The local farmers promised to take scouting trips to Yangcheng to see what had happened.

The next night a farmer reported he had seen columns of Japanese soldiers dressed in khaki uniforms with packs on their backs marching toward the east gate of Yangcheng. A week later, another farmer reported seeing them all marching out the west gate. Gladys smiled at his report. The Japanese had indeed passed through Yangcheng. Gladys's plan had worked. It would be only a matter of time before Gladys and the others could go back home.

Several members of the group were anxious to find out whether the Japanese had done any more damage to their homes and whether any of their relatives had made it back to town. Gladys volunteered to creep back into Yangcheng and see what was happening there. It took her most of the day to sneak back. She kept a lookout at every turn for men in khaki uniforms, but she saw none.

Gladys reached Yangcheng in the late afternoon. Long shadows stretched down the mountainside as she crept through the west gate. No people were gathered by the gate to sell cloth and vegetables, no gate keeper was waving as she entered, and no laughing children were running through the streets. An eerie silence hung over the once bustling town, now deserted. Gladys didn't want to stay in Yangcheng a minute longer than she had to.

Gladys quickly made her way to the Inn of Eight Happinesses and picked her way silently through its mangled remains. She sat on the edge of the k'ang. For a moment, the room echoed in her mind with the laughter of the muleteers, the songs of the new converts, and the "elastic" Bible stories Yang had told. But all of that was gone now, swept away by the evil of war. A piece of paper on the floor caught Gladys's attention. She bent to pick it up. It was a card she'd written seven years before to Mrs. Lawson, dated a week before her friend had died. It read, "I can do all things through God who strengthens me."

As Gladys tucked the card into her jacket pocket, she heard a terrifying sound: gunfire, and lots of it. She heard yelling, too. Not yelling in Chinese but in Japanese. Gladys lowered herself to the floor and lay completely still. One of two things must have happened, she decided. Either the Japanese troops had not all left town after all, or they had come back! Whichever it was, Gladys knew she had to get out of town without delay. Slowly she stood up, took a deep breath to control her shaking, and began creeping towards the east gate, the closest gate to the inn. She stayed in the shadows. But when she got within sight of the east gate, her heart sank. The gate was bolted shut. The only way out of Yangcheng was through the west gate.

Gladys checked to make sure the way was clear. This time she didn't creep along in the shadows. She stepped out into the middle of the battle-scarred street and ran as fast as she could towards the west gate. She was gasping for breath when the west gate came into view. Although the gate was still open, she suddenly knew she should be cautious. Gladys stopped running and began inching her way along in the shadows again. She was about five feet from the gate when she froze. Gunfire was exploding so close to her she could feel its vibrations as it hit the wall. She looked around in a panic. Was someone shooting at her? Her eyes drifted upwards. To her surprise, on top of the wall were eight Nationalist Chinese soldiers with their rifles pointed out over the wall. Gladys had no idea that any Nationalist troops were left in the area.

Gladys fell to her hands and knees and crawled along until she could peer through the crack between the edge of the wall and the gate. Outside the wall and to the left she caught a glimpse of Japanese uniforms and rifle barrels jutting out from behind some rocks. The sun was setting, and Gladys didn't know what to do. She was sure the soldiers would close the gate at any moment to keep the Japanese out. But being trapped inside Yangcheng would be very dangerous. She had no choice. She was going to have to sneak out through the gate in the midst of the gunfight.

Gladys peered through the crack again. To the right and about five yards outside the wall was a wheat field. The spring crop was almost two feet tall, and Gladys decided that if she could make it that far, she could crawl through the wheat without being seen. Her one advantage was that the

Japanese wouldn't be expecting anyone to flee out the gate.

Once Gladys made up her mind to run, it was only a matter of timing. All she had to do was wait for some sort of distraction and then run as hard as she could. Her heart beat so loudly she wondered whether the soldiers above could hear it. She waited. Suddenly she saw a hand grenade being lobbed over the wall towards the Japanese. This was her chance. With all her might, she sprinted out the gate and dove face first into the wheat. Quickly she pulled herself along on her elbows towards the center of the field. The wheat stalks stabbed at her, and the rocks ripped at her elbows and knees as she wormed her way towards safety.

Gladys scrambled on, staying low against the setting sun, until she finally felt safe enough to stand up. She dusted herself off, found the mule trail, and followed it a short distance until she came to a fork. One branch, which was used in bad weather, carved a steep path along the top of the mountain. It would be a dangerous route to travel at night. If she slipped and fell, Gladys knew it was unlikely her body would ever be found. The other path, the safer path, followed a stream bed that overflowed with water in the rainy season. But it was spring, and the stream bed was dry. Gladys took a few steps along this trail before she stopped in her tracks. A horrible thought occurred to her. If more Japanese soldiers were on their way back to Yangcheng, the trail she was on was the one they would almost certainly use. But she had nowhere to hide along this trail. There were no trees or rocky outcrops to conceal her. She immediately knew that despite the danger, she had to take the other trail.

She felt in her pocket for the card she'd picked from the floor of the inn. She squeezed the card, thought about the words written on it, and took a deep breath. Then she turned around and headed for the other branch of the trail.

As fast as she could, she climbed the steep path that zigzagged along the ridge. She'd gone about half a mile up the trail, when below her she heard a crunching sound. It was soft at first, but then it grew louder. Gladys recognized the sound of hundreds of boots marching over rocks. She lay down against a rock and peered over the edge of the ridge into the dusky darkness. She could make out the shape of soldiers on the move. Had Gladys stayed on the other trail, she would have walked right into these Japanese soldiers with glistening bayonets at the ends of their rifles.

Gladys spent the night huddled in the crevice of rock, high on the ridge above the gorge the soldiers had marched through. In the morning, she completed her journey back to Bei Chai Chuang. The news she reported was grim. It would not be wise to go back to Yangcheng for quite some time. They would have to stay longer in the caves.

Over the next few weeks, a steady trickle of sick and wounded people found their way to the cave of Ai-weh-deh. The people knew that Gladys would

nurse them and give them food. By the end of a
month, the cave had been transformed into a hospital. Gladys made visits to the nearby villages, where
groups of Christians were staying. She also made
several trips back to Yangcheng, where the mandarin and some residents had drifted back and reset-
tled. Even though the Japanese troops seemed to
have forgotten about the town, Gladys didn't feel it
was safe enough yet for her to return permanently.

As 1939 began, an uneasy peace settled over the
Yangcheng district. Although not many mule trains
made it through from Tsechow, many things had
returned to a familiar pattern. That is, until news
filtered back that the Japanese army was on the
march again and headed towards Yangcheng. This
time, however, the Nationalist Chinese Army had a
plan, although the plan was almost as terrifying as
another Japanese invasion. The army instructed the
mandarins throughout the area to follow what they
called a "scorched-earth" policy.

Gladys listened in horror as the mandarin
explained to her what the policy meant. "We have
been instructed to flee into the hills and leave nothing behind that the Japanese would find useful."

Gladys frowned. "Nothing?"

"Yes," the mandarin nodded sadly. "Nothing is
to be left behind. The animals that cannot be moved
are to be slaughtered, and the crops are to be
burned in the fields."

"But what about the people?" Gladys asked.
"Their crops are the only thing that will stop them

from starving to death during the winter, and it's almost harvest time."

The mandarin looked grim. "I know it is difficult. But if we leave nothing of any value for the Japanese, they will not stay here. Where will they get food or shelter?"

"Shelter?" echoed Gladys.

"Yes, shelter," he replied. "We have also been instructed to destroy the roof of every building within the city walls. The Japanese are not to be allowed a single place where they can find shelter for their troops along the way."

Gladys shook her head with despair. It seemed amazing to her that the Chinese National government would ask these people who had been through so much to destroy their last few possessions.

Finally Gladys sighed. "Perhaps they are right. Who is to know what to do these days?"

The mandarin sat down beside her. How different their meetings were now than a year ago. He had been the high and exalted one in the district, and she had been the humble foot inspector. Now they sat as equals, both caught in a web of destruction and violence beyond anything either of them could have imagined.

"I have one particular worry," the mandarin continued. "It is the Pagoda of the Scorpion."

Gladys frowned as she pictured the pagoda, an ugly building near the north wall of town. No one she recalled lived in it, and she couldn't imagine why anyone would be particularly concerned about pulling off its roof. "What is the problem?" she inquired.

"It's said that many hundreds of years ago a giant scorpion roamed the hills of Yangcheng. He killed many people, and one day the townspeople decided to trap the scorpion. The story goes that while the scorpion was asleep, the townspeople brought stones and built a pagoda over him. When he woke up he was trapped, and he has been trapped in the pagoda ever since. It became known as the Pagoda of the Scorpion. As a result, I cannot get anyone to pull the roof off the pagoda, because they're convinced they would be letting out the giant scorpion."

"But surely you don't believe that?" asked Gladys.

"No, I do not," said the mandarin with a sad smile. "But you Christians would do me a huge favor if you would agree to pull the pagoda roof down, since I have not found anyone willing to do it. Everyone else is too afraid of the scorpion."

"It would be our pleasure," Gladys assured him.

"And," the mandarin went on, "I wish to invite you to a feast. I have no doubt it will be the last feast I will host in Yangcheng, and I have one last thing to say that I particularly want you to hear."

Gladys nodded. These were sorrowful days for China.

The next day as she and some of the Christians from Bei Chai Chuang ripped the Pagoda of the Scorpion apart, Gladys wondered what it was the mandarin was anxious to say. She found out soon enough.

Gladys was welcomed into the yamen and told to sit in the seat of honor at the right of the mandarin. She had never sat there before, but it gave her a good view of all the other guests. She noted that all the important people of Yangcheng were present.

The meal was a simple one, much more like one Yang would have served to the muleteers than the elaborate dinners the mandarin had given when times were good. When the meal was almost over, the mandarin pushed his bowl aside and stood to speak.

"You came to this feast today because I invited you, and I have something very important to tell you," he began. "It has been nearly ten years since Ai-weh-deh first came into our lives. How well I remember the first time we met. I went to her house to ask for her help with the foot-binding problem, and she agreed to be my foot inspector. That was the first of many things Ai-weh-deh has done for me."

Gladys felt her face growing hot with embarrassment as the mandarin spoke. The mandarin continued for about twenty minutes, listing all the things that Gladys had done for the city, such as stopping the prison riot, improving the prisons, attending births, adopting unwanted children, being a special advisor to the mandarin. The list went on and on. Gladys thought it would have made a fine speech for her funeral, but she couldn't imagine the point of it while she was still alive.

Finally, the mandarin of Yangcheng seemed to run out of things to say. Very deliberately, he turned to Gladys and looked her directly in the eye. "Ai-weh-deh, my dear friend, Ai-weh-deh," he said. "I have seen all that you are and all that you do, and I would like to become a Christian like you."

A gasp of astonishment rose from the guests, but Gladys did not make a sound. She could not. She was too stunned. In the midst of all the violence and war, God had been quietly working in the heart of the mandarin. Tears of gratitude welled in Gladys's eyes. Whatever happened to her next, it would be worth it just to have heard the mandarin ask to become a Christian.

Chapter 13

Read by Millions of People

Gladys wound the bandage around and around Francis's hand. Then she patted her adopted son on the shoulder. "It's looking better than last week," she said kindly. "In two or three more weeks, you'll be able to take the bandages off and learn how to use your hand again." She tried to sound cheerful for her son's sake, but inside Gladys was feeling very weary.

The war had been dragging on for nearly a year and half now, and the scorched-earth policy had only seemed to make things worse. Every time the Japanese army marched into a village that had been deliberately destroyed, terrible consequences followed. Airplanes would fly low over the area, dropping bombs and machine-gunning anything that moved.

That was how Francis came to have his right hand bandaged. He had heard the buzz of aircraft and started running as fast as he could towards the cave, but he hadn't been quick enough. A burst of machine-gun fire peppered the ground around him. He was hit in the hand, and three of his fingers were blown off.

Many others in the district lost much more than their fingers. One such person was Hsi-Lien, the first muleteer ever to stay at the Inn of Eight Happinesses. Hsi-Lien had untangled his hand from the reins and fled the night Gladys dragged his mules into the courtyard of the inn. Yang had gone after him and convinced him to return. From that time on, Hsi-Lien had stayed at the inn whenever he was passing through Yangcheng. He had also become a strong Christian.

One day as Gladys was dressing the wound of an injured person in her makeshift hospital, she heard a commotion at the entrance to the cave. She turned to see what it was, and a joyful smile spread over her face when she saw Hsi-Lien.

"Welcome, Hsi-Lien. It is an honor to have you visit us," Gladys called out.

As she walked over to him, she sensed something was very wrong. He looked like the Hsi-Lien she knew, but he wasn't acting like him. Instead of excitedly greeting Gladys as he usually did, he just stood at the cave entrance, staring. His eyes looked sad and dull, and though his lips moved, no sound came out of his mouth.

"What is it, my friend?" asked Gladys. "Come and have tea with me." She took him by the arm and led him over to where a pot of water was boiling over an open fire.

They sat on some rocks, and Gladys dropped some leaves from a nearby bush into the water. The mixture tasted nothing like tea, but it was the best they could do in such trying times, and it warmed their stomachs. As they sipped the tea, Gladys spoke soothingly to Hsi-Lien. Then slowly and painfully his story came out.

Hsi-Lien lived in Chowtsun, halfway between Yangcheng and Tsechow. As they had done with Yangcheng, Japanese soldiers had invaded his town. When the Japanese finally found out he was a muleteer, they ordered him to prepare his mule train to carry ammunition and guns for them. But Hsi-Lien refused. He explained to the Japanese that he was a Christian man and would not carry weapons to be used to kill his fellow men.

At first the soldiers laughed at him, thinking once he understood they were serious, he would gladly carry their weapons. But they were wrong, and Hsi-Lien continued to refuse to carry guns and ammunition on his mules.

Gladys poured some more tea into Hsi-Lien's cup. "Go on," she urged. "What happened next?"

"Once they saw I was serious, they dragged me outside my house and tied me to a wooden stake."

That's it, thought Gladys. No wonder Hsi-Lien is so upset. He was badly tortured by the Japanese.

Hsi-Lien grew silent for a long time, as though he were drawing the courage to go on with his story.

"I thought they were going to torture me," he finally went on, "but they did not touch me. Instead they began to board up the doors and windows of my house. My wife and children were inside…" his voice trailed off.

Gladys put her hand on his shoulder for comfort.

"Fire," he said in a whisper. "They set the house on fire."

Gladys wiped away the tears that were now falling down her cheeks.

"Later some neighbors untied me, but there was nothing left. They are all gone. All gone." With his tale told, Hsi-Lien sat in silence, staring at the ground.

There was nothing Gladys could do to undo the terrible evil the Japanese had inflicted on such a kind and gentle man as Hsi-Lien, but she could make sure his family received a Christian burial. She and some of the Christians from Bei Chai Chuang went to Chowtsun and pulled the charred remains of Hsi-Lien's family from the rubble of the house. They dug a large grave in the cemetery, said prayers, sang a hymn, and buried the bodies. Hsi-Lien was grateful for their help, but he never fully recovered. For the rest of his life, he spent long periods of time staring aimlessly, and sometimes he would go for days without talking.

The war was horrible. Not a day went by without somebody else arriving at Gladys's cave with a sad story to tell, just like Hsi-Lien's. China was in an uproar. The Nationalist soldiers were fighting their old enemy, the Communists, who had been trying to seize control of China for a number of years, and both armies were trying to rid the country of the Japanese. As the war went on, thousands of children were either separated from their parents or orphaned. From over a hundred miles away, some of these children found their way to Ai-weh-deh. They had heard she would take care of them. And she did.

Gladys gave up counting at one hundred fifty children, but still they flowed in. Each day was a strain to find enough food and clothing for them all. Eventually the good news that the Japanese had retreated from Yangcheng all the way back to Tsechow reached Gladys and the children at the cave. Gladys satisfied herself that the report was true and moved back to the Inn of Eight Happinesses with the children. Most of the other citizens of Yangcheng who had survived the war also trickled back. Sadly, Gladys's old friend the mandarin was no longer there. In an attempt to consolidate their control over the area, the Japanese had captured many mandarins and executed them. To avoid capture, the mandarin had fled Yangcheng with his family soon after he'd become a Christian.

Some major repairs needed to be made to the inn. The walls had to be shored up, and a replacement roof had to be constructed, not to mention a new floor upstairs. Soon the old building was filled with life and the voices of children.

Once the repairs to the inn were made, Gladys set out to visit the mission in Tsechow and see whether she could do anything to help David and Jean Davies. She had been worried about them; they were housing hundreds of refugees from outlying areas.

When she arrived, Gladys found she needn't have worried. The couple told her that the Japanese soldiers had been very well behaved in Tsechow and had not killed or tortured anyone. They always had candies in their pockets for the children, and many of them came to the mission's church meetings. To the Davieses, the Japanese were nothing to be afraid of. That is, until one dark, moonless night soon after Gladys arrived.

Gladys had gone to bed early and was fast asleep by midnight when the screams began. She awoke with a start, and when she realized the screams were coming from the single-women refugees' dormitory, she leapt out of bed and raced from the room. She ran to the dormitory and swung the door open. Inside were about fifty Japanese soldiers, yelling and poking guns at the terrified women. Some of them were ripping off the women's clothes. Gladys took a deep breath and charged into the room. A Japanese soldier saw her coming and drew his rifle back. Gladys was about five feet into the room when the soldier brought the butt of his rifle down as hard as he could on the side of her head. There was a sickening thud as Gladys collapsed unconscious to the floor, with blood flowing from the gash in her head. It was several hours before Gladys regained consciousness, and when she did, Jean Davies told her what had happened.

David Davies had also heard the screams. He arrived at the women's dormitory just as Gladys was hit over the head. He knew he could do nothing to fend off fifty armed men, so he yelled for all the women to pray. A few of them heard him and fell to their knees. A soldier swung his rifle butt at David, catching him across the cheek, ripping it open. As David sank to his knees, he kept yelling, "Pray, pray."

This made the soldier who had hit him very angry. The soldier aimed his rifle at David's head and pulled the trigger. The gun didn't fire. He pulled the trigger again. The gun still didn't fire. The soldier started pulling the trigger frantically, but his rifle would not fire. Finally he removed his gun from David's head and backed out the door with great fear.

Meanwhile, the women were doing as they had been told. One by one, they fell to their knees and prayed. The soldiers didn't know what to do. This attack was unlike any other they had made. While the soldiers were arguing among themselves over what to do next, their captain arrived and ordered them all back to barracks.

"Did any of the women get hurt?" asked Gladys.

Jean Davies shook her head, "Not one. And David will be okay, too. He had to have a lot of stitches in his cheek, though."

Gladys sank into her pillow, hoping the war would soon be over. But things got worse. While she was away from Yangcheng, Less, her oldest son, had joined the Nationalist Chinese Army. Within a few weeks of his signing up, Gladys received the sad news that he'd been killed in the fighting.

Several months after the incident in Tsechow, Gladys had an opportunity to tell others what was happening in China. Theodore White, an American freelance journalist, had found his way to Shansi province. Once he arrived, everyone told him about a little English woman who was helping refugees in the mountains. Her name was Ai-weh-deh, and just about everyone he met told him he should interview her. Theodore White decided to take their advice and find this Ai-weh-deh.

He found Gladys in Yangcheng surrounded by orphans, bombing victims, and new converts. He was amazed at the work she was doing and at her choice to stay in a war zone instead of fleeing to safety. Theodore White asked Gladys many questions, which she gladly answered. Gladys hoped that what he wrote would be published so that people could read about the problems in China. She never dreamed the story would be published in one of the largest news magazines in the world: *Time* magazine. *Time* bought and printed Theodore White's article about Gladys, and it was read by millions of people all over the United States and Great Britain and around the world.

Throughout this time, Gladys kept busy with her missionary work in the small villages surrounding Yangcheng. She traveled from village to village, encouraging the Christian converts and praying with them. The Chinese Army general stationed in the area decided that Gladys probably knew more than anyone else about Japanese troop movements in the countryside. He asked Gladys to tell him which way the Japanese soldiers were headed whenever she saw them. He also wanted to know how the soldiers were treating the local people. Gladys was glad to do this if it would help get the Japanese out of China. Without really ever using the word, Gladys knew she had become a spy for her adopted homeland.

The general began to ask Gladys questions about her work. He could hardly believe it when she told him she had nearly two hundred children in her care. He couldn't understand how she fed them all each day. Gladys couldn't explain it either, but somehow she was able to feed them all. The general told Gladys he'd heard there were many orphanages in Shensi province set up by Madame Chiang Kai-shek, the wife of the leader of the Chinese Nationalist government. The government had taken over colleges and temples and turned them into orphanages for some of the millions of children who had been orphaned by the brutal fighting. The general suggested that Gladys write to

Madame Chiang and see whether she could find room in an orphanage for the children. Gladys wrote the letter, and the general saw that it was delivered.

A month later a messenger arrived with a letter for Gladys from Madame Chiang Kai-shek. Gladys ripped the letter open and read it. The letter said that if Gladys could find a way to get the children to Sian in Shensi province, Madame Chiang would find a place for them in orphanages. She would also send money back to help Gladys with her work in Yangcheng.

It all sounded straightforward. Shensi was the next province to Shansi, across the Yellow River to the west. One of the new converts, Tsin Pen-kuang, offered to escort the first hundred children to Sian. He would also collect the money for Gladys and bring it back. Then he would make another trip to Sian with the rest of the children. That way, all the children would be safe, and Gladys would be free to stay and work among the people of the district.

Gladys hugged every one of the hundred children good-bye and promised to pray for them until she heard they were safe in Sian. The children had a long journey ahead of them. It was more than two hundred miles from Yangcheng to Sian. The children would travel over mountain trails and have to cross the Yellow River. The whole journey would take them about fourteen days, and along the way, farmers would help to feed them. But long as the trip was, Gladys knew it would be worth it for the children. They would be moving away from the war zone and would be much safer in Sian.

Once they had left, Gladys waited impatiently for word they'd arrived safely. Five weeks later, to her relief, word came that the children had all made it to Sian. Now Gladys anxiously waited for Tsin Pen-kuang to return for the rest of the children. Gladys promised herself she would go to Sian when the war was over and visit all of the children. In the meantime, she had much to do. The Christian converts in the area continued to need support and encouragement, as did most of the people in Yangcheng. And then there were the sick and the wounded, who needed to be tended to and cared for.

As Gladys waited anxiously for Tsin Pen-kuang to return and take the second group of children to Sian, two very important things occurred that she didn't know about. Tsin Pen-kuang wouldn't be coming back for the other children, ever. He had been robbed and killed by Japanese soldiers on the return journey. And a copy of the *Time* magazine article about Gladys by Theodore White had fallen into the hands of the Japanese. Ai-weh-deh was a marked woman.

Chapter 14

A Price on Her Head

A hail of small pebbles pinged against the rice paper screen in the window of Gladys's room. Gladys's heart beat loudly as she lay still, trying to decide what to do. Finally, she called out to see who was trying to get her attention. Much to her relief, it was a Nationalist Chinese soldier. He was a Christian, and Gladys knew him well. She slipped on her jacket and went downstairs to let him in.

As she closed the door behind him, he looked around nervously. "You must come with the soldiers," he began. "The Japanese are coming back, and we do not have enough men to hold them off. We are leaving Yangcheng, and it will fall back into enemy hands. The Japanese are becoming more desperate. You will not be safe here. You must come with me now. The general orders you to. The children can come, too. He has sent you a letter."

The soldier thrust a large sheet of parchment into Gladys's hand. Gladys held the paper close to the lamp and read it. It echoed what the soldier had just told her. As she read, anger rose in her. Who did the general think he was to give her orders? She might be his spy, but she most certainly wasn't in his army. She was under God's orders, and no one else's! So Gladys took a pen, and with a flourish, she wrote "chi tao tu pu twai" (Christians never retreat) on the back of the letter and signed it. Feeling pleased at having made her point loud and clear, she handed the letter back to the soldier and told him to give it to the general.

The soldier shook his head. "You don't understand. You must come. You are in great danger," he pleaded.

"Rubbish," replied Gladys, ignoring the fact she had gone to bed with the same impression only an hour or so before. "I am a Chinese citizen, just like everyone else who is going to stay. So I am in the same danger as anyone else in Yangcheng. No more and no less. I would be grateful, though, if you would take the children with you to safety, but I will stay here where I can do the most good."

Shaking his head at Gladys's reply, the soldier pulled a second sheet of paper from his pocket and handed it to Gladys. He spoke gently. "I do not mean to scare you, Ai-weh-deh, but you are mistaken. These are already posted on every side of the city wall in Tsechow and will be on the city wall of Yangcheng as soon as the Japanese arrive."

Gladys unfolded the paper and held it close to the lamp. It was a poster with "Reward" written in large letters across the top. Then the poster read: "Any person who gives information that leads to the capture (dead or alive) of the below mentioned people will receive a one hundred dollar reward from the Japanese High Command." Three names were listed on the poster. Gladys knew them all. The first was the mandarin of Tsechow. The second was a well-known businessman in the region. The third name read, "Ai-weh-deh, also known as the Small Woman."

Gladys stared at the poster as if she expected her name to disappear at any moment. The soldier interrupted her thoughts. "The general said the Japanese found some news article from America. You said bad things about them in it. They will have no mercy when they find you."

Gladys tried to let the information sink in. She had a price on her head, and a large one at that. Everyone within a hundred miles of Yangcheng knew who she was, and one of them, she felt sure, would give in to the temptation to make easy money off that knowledge. She needed some time to think about what to do.

"Thank you," she said to the soldier. "I will tell you my decision in the morning."

The soldier bowed and disappeared into the darkness. With trembling hands, Gladys bolted the door behind him.

An important choice lay in front of her. Should she run away or stay and face possible torture and death? Gladys didn't shrink at the idea of staying, yet she wondered whether there would be any point to her dying at the hands of the Japanese. She thought of a Chinese prayer Mrs. Lawson had taught her years ago. "If I must die, let me not be afraid of death, but let there be a meaning, O God, in my dying."

Quietly, so as not to disturb any of the children, Gladys carried the lamp back to her bedroom. "O God," she prayed, "show me what to do." With that, she picked up her Bible and opened it. She ran her finger over the Chinese characters printed on the page and then stopped. She read the verse her finger was on. "Flee ye! Flee ye into the mountains! Dwell deeply in the hidden places, because the King of Babylon has conceived a purpose against you!"

Gladys had her answer. Sometimes Christians should retreat, and Gladys believed from the verse she'd just read that this was one of those times. As she lay awake that night, Gladys knew she had to lead the children to safety in Sian herself. It was no use waiting any longer for Tsin Pen-kuang to return. Something must have happened to him, or he would have been back weeks ago. She could take the general up on his offer to protect her and the children. But if the Chinese Nationalist soldiers were forced to flee the advancing Japanese, what kind of protection could they really offer? Gladys had to face facts. She was right in the middle of a war zone. If the Japanese found her with ninety-four children, they would probably first kill the children right in front of her just before they killed her.

As the first rays of sunlight reached in through her rice paper window, Gladys set her plan in motion. She woke all the children and told them to put on every piece of clothing that they owned and tie any spare cloth shoes they had around their waists. Gladys knew that shoes would be a problem on the journey. The shoes were made of cloth with bark for soles and were expected to last only a month or so around the village streets. Over the rough rocks and narrow mountain tracks they would be following, a pair of shoes would barely last a day.

Once the children were dressed, Gladys had them gather up their bedrolls and line up in order of size, girls on one side, boys on the other. The line stretched out the door and across the courtyard. Gladys surveyed the scene. At the front of the girls' line, she counted twenty girls who were thirteen to fifteen years old, including Ninepence. These older girls would be helpful in controlling the little ones, as would the seven older boys from eleven to fifteen. The remaining sixty-seven children were all too young to be helpful to anyone. The youngest was barely four years old, but she would have to be responsible for her own bedroll, just like everyone else.

Gladys gathered up the remaining food supply in the house, enough millet for two days, and wrapped it in a rag, which she gave to one of the older boys to carry. She carried the iron pot herself to cook the millet in.

The procession wound its way through the west gate of Yangcheng for the last time. Only a few of the older children had any idea of the danger that lay ahead of them. To the little ones, it was a chance to run and play in the open air. They chattered and giggled, running ahead and ambushing the main group, climbing plum trees, and scurrying from the front of the line to the back with silly messages for each other. It was only as the afternoon wore on that a few of them asked Gladys where they were going to sleep that night. Gladys had no idea. She had never taken the route to the Yellow River before. Some of the muleteers had told her it took five days on the main trails to reach the river, so she estimated it would take about twelve days to reach it going over the mountains on less-traveled trails.

The children were becoming hungry and tired when the first village appeared in the distance. Gladys encouraged them on, and as the sun began to set, they entered the village. Gladys walked near the front of the group, and as she turned to see the straggling line of children behind her, she wondered where nearly a hundred children would find shelter.

As if in answer to her question, she looked up and saw a Buddhist priest, dressed in his saffron robes, standing on the steps of a temple. "Where are you going with all those children?" he asked.

"To Sian. We are refugees," replied Gladys.

The priest looked puzzled. "Are they all yours?" he asked.

"Yes," said Gladys, too tired to explain further. "I need a place for us to sleep tonight."

"Well, I don't see why you can't sleep in the temple. There is plenty of room on the floor," he said as he waved the children inside.

Gladys was grateful for a roof over their heads. In the open courtyard over a fire, she boiled millet for everyone. After eating, the children unrolled their bedrolls and promptly fell asleep. Sleep didn't come so easily for Gladys, however. For one thing, rats were scurrying in every corner. More serious than that, though, Gladys was beginning to have nagging doubts about whether they could make it to Sian or not. Today was the easiest day, and it had proved difficult enough. Some of the older girls, whom she was relying on, were not walking well. Their feet had been bound earlier in their lives, and although they had now been unbound for many years, they were not strong and flat like normal feet.

And then there was the food supply. The millet they had with them could be stretched to last only a couple of days. After that, where would they find enough food each day to feed nearly a hundred people? And although the little ones were still filled with enthusiasm, what about when they began to lag behind? There weren't enough older children to piggyback them all. And Gladys wouldn't even allow herself to dwell on the worst possibility of all—meeting Japanese soldiers. When Tsin Pen-kuang had taken the first hundred children to Sian, there had been little Japanese activity in the area. But lately, according to the priest, there had been many sightings of soldiers in the area. If the children were found with Ai-weh-deh, the woman on the wanted poster, there would be no mercy shown to any of them.

The next morning, the children obediently rolled up their bedrolls, ate their bowl of millet, thanked the Buddhist priest for his help, and marched out into the countryside once more. The next night they spent squeezed into a house, and the two nights after that were spent out in the open. On the fifth day, they began to trek over the mountains. They were walking along small tracks that kept forking into two tracks, and each time they came to a fork, Gladys looked at the sun and calculated which way was southwest. That was the track they took. By the fifth night, the laughing, carefree group that had left Yangcheng was nowhere to be seen. In its place was a group of older girls with cut and bruised feet, older boys struggling under the burden of piles of bedrolls, and little four- and five-year-olds who cried when they were hungry and cried when they were scared, which meant there were ten or twelve of them wailing together at any one time. Gladys herself was feeling a strange tiredness. She'd felt it often since being struck in the head with the rifle butt in Tsechow. Sometimes more than anything, she just wanted to curl up under a rock and sleep, even in the middle of the day. But with the lives of so many children depending on her, she wouldn't give in to the fatigue.

Sometimes the children sang hymns as they walked, and sometimes they trudged on in silence, except for the crying children. It was during one of the quiet times that two of the older boys who had been sent on ahead to scout the trail came rushing back. "Soldiers," they yelled.

Gladys clutched the hands of the nearest children. Her eyes darted from side to side. Gladys and the children were in a narrow ravine, and there was nowhere for them to all get off the track. For a sickening moment, Gladys was unsure of what to tell the children to do next. Then she heard a voice in the distance. The voice spoke Chinese, not Japanese. Gladys's grip on the children relaxed. The soldiers coming were friends not enemies. Gladys and the children stood waiting as the soldiers came closer. Just as the soldiers came into view, the sound of airplanes was heard above. Everyone looked up, and overhead were the shimmering silver underbellies of Japanese bombers. The children and the approaching soldiers instinctively dove for cover under trees and rocks.

Gladys crouched under a bush, huddled over three of the smallest children, waiting tensely for the hail of machine-gun bullets or the bombs that always seemed to accompany Japanese airplanes. This time there was no attack. Because of the steep, rocky ravine, the pilots hadn't spotted the escaping people. Once the planes were out of sight, the children and soldiers crawled from their hiding places and greeted each other. They were glad to see each other, the soldiers no doubt because they were a long way from their own children, and the children because the soldiers' knapsacks were filled with sugar treats and food the children had not seen for many months in Shansi province.

Since it was nearly nightfall, the soldiers invited Gladys and the children to spend the night around the campfire with them. They provided a feast for the children, and for the first time on the journey, Gladys felt free to eat her share of food. They all slept well that night. Early the next morning, both groups wished each other well and set out in opposite directions.

In the following days, Gladys often thought of the meal they had eaten with the Nationalist soldiers. She and the children hadn't eaten since. Now to sustain them they had only hot tea made by boiling twigs and leaves they picked along the way. They sipped the brew from the few rice bowls that had not been broken or lost.

The sun beat down during the day, cracking the children's lips and sapping their energy, and at night, the howl of wolves filled them with terror. But they plodded on, making more and more frequent stops, and looking around every bend in the path for a glimpse of the mighty Yellow River in the distance. Gladys had told them that once they saw it, they would soon be out of the mountains, and once across the river, they could ride on something called a train the rest of the way to Sian.

By the twelfth day, the journey had become almost unbearable. The little ones no longer laughed or showed any of the silliness they had exhibited on the first day of their march. Now everyone concentrated on the grim task of placing one cut and blistered foot in front of the other. Gladys worried that if any more Japanese planes flew overhead, none of them would have the energy to hide. But still they trudged on. At midday, Gladys noticed they were no longer climbing. In fact, the trail was beginning to head downward, out of the mountains. And then Gladys saw what they had been waiting so long to see—the Yellow River, glistening in the distance.

"Come on, children, that is where we are going," yelled Gladys, pointing towards the river.

"But it is so far away," replied one of the children.

"The rocks are hurting my feet," complained another.

"We'll never make it that far," stated a third.

"Of course we can make it," said Gladys. "Look down there." She pointed to a small village between them and the river. "I think that is Yuan Chu. We will find food there, and then it is a short walk to the river. We'll get a boat across, and before nightfall we will be eating delicious hot soup, and then we'll sleep on a warm k'ang tonight."

This thought cheered the children up. Along with the fact that the trail now led steadily downhill, they all walked a little faster and began to sing hymns as they had done on the first few days of the trek.

Two hours later, nearly a hundred hymn-singing children with shredded shoes and cracked lips straggled through the gates of Yuan Chu. They expected to be met by the local people, but none were there. The children yelled and opened gates into private courtyards. They peered into the temple and looked in the marketplace, but not a person was in sight.

Finally, one of the children saw an old man asleep under a tree. She went to fetch Gladys, who hurried off in the old man's direction, hoping he was indeed asleep and not dead. By the time she reached him, he had been awakened by the children's noise and was grumbling about it.

Gladys began the conversation. "We are in Yuan Chu, aren't we?"

"Yes," replied the old man.

"Then where is everyone?" Gladys asked.

"Gone. The Japanese are coming, and everyone has crossed the river."

"Why didn't you go with them?" she asked.

"I am too old, and they have already killed my sons. I would rather use my last breath to spit on the Japanese than to run from them," the old man snarled.

"How did everyone get across the river?" Gladys asked, changing the subject.

"Boats took them, but they're all gone now. There are no more boats on the river. You came from the mountains, you had better go back to the mountains, otherwise you will be trapped. Then the Japanese will kill you all."

Gladys sighed deeply. She couldn't take the children back into the mountains. There was no food there, and they would certainly starve to death. So with more confidence than she felt, she declared, "We are going to Sian. We have walked for twelve days, and we will not stop now. We will walk to the river, and we will find a way to get across. God will help us."

The old man spat on the ground. "You are a fool. You might escape on your own when the Japanese come, but with this army of children, you don't have a chance."

Gladys whistled loudly, and all the children came scurrying from the various deserted houses and inns. "Come on," she called. "We are nearly at the river." Gladys scooped up one of the little boys to carry him piggyback. As she walked, she wondered how they would get across the Yellow River. Had she led the children all this way for nothing? What would she do with ninety-four children if they couldn't go back and they could not go forward?

Chapter 15

As Black as the Night

For four days, Gladys and the children sat by the riverbank. They had waded in the shallow waters of the mile-wide Yellow River, but they had not crossed it. The old man at Yuan Chu had been right, there was not a boat anywhere to ferry them across. On their first day at the river's edge, Gladys had sent the oldest boys back to Yuan Chu to scavenge for food. The boys had found some stale cakes and a couple of pounds of half-rotten millet. Gladys had boiled it all in the kettle and ladled the soup out to the younger children. That was the last food any of them had eaten.

As they waited by the river, Gladys could feel herself slipping in and out of consciousness. Her only clear thought was that she needed to get the children to Sian. Other than that, everything became blurry and unreal to her.

The children were asking her questions. "Why can't we walk on water like Jesus?" and "Ai-weh-deh, why can't you part the Yellow River like Moses did?"

Gladys had no response other than to urge the tired, hungry children to sing hymns and pray. The hymn singing became the answer to their prayers.

A Nationalist Chinese soldier stood on the crest of the hill overlooking the peculiar sight of a large circle of dirty, thin children singing loudly. One of the younger children spotted him and raced up the hill, no doubt remembering the other Chinese soldiers who had shared candy with them two weeks before. Gladys looked up to see what all the excitement was about. Was that a soldier she saw? She couldn't be sure. Two of the children ran up and pulled her to her feet. She swayed slightly and peered, and soon, the face of a soldier came into focus.

"I heard the singing," said the soldier. "Who are you, and what are you doing here?"

"We are refugees on our way to Sian, and we need to cross the river," said Gladys, too tired to think about where the soldier had come from or what he might be doing there.

"How many of you are there?" he asked.

"Ninety-four," Gladys replied, as she sat down again. Standing made her feel dizzy.

"Are you sick?" asked the soldier, when he saw she could not stand.

Gladys shook her head. "I'll be fine when I get the children to Sian. Can you help us cross the river?"

The soldier looked slowly around at the children. "Yes," he said quietly. "I will help you, but it will be dangerous. The Japanese are not far away. If they fly over while we are in the boat, they will shoot us all. They have no mercy." He stopped and looked once again at the smallest children playing in the reeds. "In fact," he went on, "they have flown over this spot every day for weeks, shooting into the reeds. This week, for the first time, they have not come here at all."

The soldier turned abruptly towards the river and let out a series of shrill whistles. Everyone watched eagerly as slowly an open wooden boat came into view. It took three trips to ferry Gladys and all of the children across the river. Thankfully, no sign of any Japanese aircraft appeared overhead.

On the other side, Gladys gathered the children to offer a prayer of thanks. The waters may not have parted like they did for Moses, but God still had provided a way across the Yellow River.

Gladys and the children spent that night in a nearby village. As usual, when the villagers saw so many children, they did their best to help, willingly sharing their precious food supplies and their k'angs.

Finally, the next morning, Gladys and the children marched to the train station. Gladys had been told that since they were refugees, she and the children could board any southbound train free of charge and the train would take them to Sian. Along the way, refugee organizations had set up food stations. When Gladys heard this, she was too overcome with relief to speak. Instead, she put her hands over her face and sobbed. Could it be true? Was the worst really behind them?

Gladys stood at the station, staring down the tracks, praying that a train would arrive. Then in the distance she saw a puff of steam. A train was coming! Gladys had tried to tell the children about a train, but none of them had ever seen any moving machine before except for an airplane, and that had been a terrifying experience for them all. The railroad tracks began to vibrate as the train roared into view, hissing and belching clouds of white steam and dark smoke. When Gladys turned to reassure the children, they were gone, all ninety-four of them! In a split second, even the oldest children had panicked and scattered in all directions. Some of the adults on the platform were laughing loudly, but it was no laughing matter to Gladys, who had ninety-four children to find before the train left. Thankfully, the engineer was not in too much of a hurry, and he waited patiently while Gladys trekked all the way back to the village gates to find some of the smallest children hiding there.

Gladys convinced the children they were not entering the bowels of a giant dragon, and they all climbed aboard. True to what she had been told, the group was not charged to ride the train. As the train pulled out from the station, Gladys laid her head against the window and drifted off to sleep. Suddenly, she was awakened by screaming. In an instant, she was sitting bolt upright in pitch darkness. It took her a moment to realize where she was, and then she smiled. The train was going through a tunnel, and the darkness had scared the children.

After three days, the children became quite used to life aboard the train. They didn't even blink at a tunnel, and they loved clambering off at some of the bigger cities to get a free meal. Gladys couldn't understand, though, why she didn't feel more refreshed as the days went on. She was getting food and rest, but it seemed to make no difference.

On the fourth day, about mid-morning, the train hissed to a stop. Everyone peered out the windows. The train stood in a rocky ravine, and there was no station nearby. Gladys felt a chill run down her spine. Something bad had happened; she knew it. And she was right. The train had stopped for one simple reason. It could go no farther. The conductor made his way through the train with the bad news. The railway bridge ahead of them had been bombed. If they wanted to get to Sian, they would have to climb over the mountain the train was winding its way around and catch a train on the railway line on the other side. Gladys sat numbly as one of the other passengers asked how long it would take to reach the other side of the mountain. She shut her eyes when she heard the reply: four or five days.

Weary, Gladys called the roll. Everyone was accounted for. Then she looked up at the steep rock face of the mountain. Could they do it? Would this nightmare journey never end? Gladys wondered whether maybe she'd done the wrong thing trying to lead the children to safety. In her attempt to save them, had she doomed them to a slow death instead of a quick one at the hands of the Japanese? As her thoughts flowed, so did the tears. She sat on a nearby rock and wept loudly. The children began to cry, too. At first, one or two of the youngest ones started, and soon everyone was crying. They made quite a racket. After several minutes, Gladys wiped her eyes on the back of her sleeve.

"That's enough," she yelled over the noise. "A good cry never harmed anyone, but now it's time to get going. Let's sing."

And sing they did; up and down mountains, along narrow tracks, and through forests they sang. It took them five days to reach Tung Kwan on the other side of the mountain. At night they slept in caves, and during the day they climbed or walked slowly, waiting for the lagging children to catch up. Gladys's constant assurance that they would find food and hot tea waiting for them on the other side of the mountain kept them moving forward.

In Tung Kwan, Gladys received yet more bad news. There were railroad tracks, and there were trains running to Sian, but they were only coal trains. The tracks were closed to all other trains. The authorities had declared the route too dangerous for passengers because the tracks ran along the banks of the Yellow River where the Japanese were bombing. There were no exceptions to their rule.

Gladys was stunned. She couldn't go on, and she knew it. For three weeks, she and the children had walked, climbed, and clawed their way over mountains, avoided Japanese planes, and begged food. The children were hungry, bleeding, and dehydrated. Their shoes had worn out, and many of them were coughing ominously. Gladys couldn't go forward, and she could not go back; she could only trust God. With that trust, she instructed the children to lay out their bedrolls on the station platform and get some sleep. Then she leaned against the wall of the station and drifted off to sleep.

Gladys woke with two men shaking her. For a moment, she thought she was back on the train station platform at Chita all those years ago. Fear gripped her, but she was too tired to care. She just wanted to be alone to sleep. "Let me alone. I want to sleep. This is a public platform, isn't it?" she said grumpily.

Within a few minutes, however, Gladys was wide awake and scrambling to her feet. She could hardly believe the good news. Evidently, one of the coal stokers on the train had seen all the sleeping children sprawled out on the platform and had inquired about them. Then he had convinced the engineer to let the children ride the coal train, right on top of the coal.

Soon the younger children were being gently passed, still sleeping, from person to person and lifted onto the tops of the coal cars. One older child was assigned to each car, and his or her job was to build a little coal wall around each sleeping child so the child wouldn't roll off the coal car when it lurched around curves. Once Gladys was satisfied that all the children were safely aboard, she too climbed onto a pile of coal.

When the little children awoke the next morning, they shrieked with delight. Everyone, even Ai-weh-deh, was as black as the night. Coal dust had settled all over them. Gladys laughed, too. It was so good to see the children happy again, and they were very well camouflaged! As long as the Japanese didn't bomb the train, they would make it to Sian in three days.

It was impossible to get comfortable sitting or lying on a pile of coal, but the children didn't complain too much. It was a lot better than hiking over mountains! The three days passed quickly, and finally the train hissed to a stop. The engineer walked back and told Gladys they were in Sian. That was the good news. The bad news was that no one was allowed off the train there. The city had been overrun with refugees, and no more people were allowed to enter the city. Guards stood on the train station platforms to make sure no one climbed off a train.

Gladys didn't know what to do. The engineer told her the city of Fufeng was three days' journey from Sian, and as far as he knew, Fufeng was still accepting refugees. Gladys wept bitterly at the news, but deep inside she found the strength to go on.

The next three days on the train were a muddled blur for Gladys. Sometimes she thought she was back in England with her parents, sometimes she hid her head in her hands when she thought she heard Japanese planes, and sometimes she thought she was standing on the banks of a wide river she could never cross. By the time they got to Fufeng, Gladys couldn't celebrate. She hardly knew where or who she was. In spite of her condition, she managed to find an orphanage that would take all the children. Within two days of delivering the children safely to the orphanage, Gladys fell into a coma. No one could wake her from it, and she was transferred to a hospital.

Chapter 16

Going Home

The voices sounded far away at first, drifting quietly through the fog in her mind. But slowly they grew louder. Gladys could begin to make out the words—English words. She opened her eyes. She was lying on a bed in a room with white walls. But where were the children? Why couldn't she hear their voices? And where was she, anyway? The last she remembered she was riding on a pile of coal on a train.

Gladys could hear the voices in English again. They were coming from beyond the curtain that surrounded her bed. A man was talking. "It's hard to believe she's only thirty-eight. She seems much older. Her body appears to be completely worn out."

Then Gladys heard a woman's voice. "It's incredible she's alive at all. Fever, pneumonia, typhoid, malnutrition. Any one of those would kill a normal person, and she was carried in here two weeks ago with all four!"

Who was talking? Gladys wanted to know. She let out a moan, and the curtain was instantly pulled back. Gladys saw a European doctor and a nurse, who hurried to her side when they realized she was conscious again.

For the next two months, Gladys faded in and out of consciousness in the hospital run by Baptist missionaries. Sometimes she didn't know who she was or what she was doing in the hospital, and she always asked the same question: "Are the children safe?" Miraculously, they were. Through the entire journey from Yangcheng, not one child had died or even become seriously ill.

Finally, Gladys was well enough for the doctor to suggest she stay with some missionary friends of his in the countryside. There she would be able to rest and recover even more.

Gladys lived in the country for several months before she felt strong enough to move out on her own again. All of the children were being taken care of in a refugee orphanage, but as soon as Gladys was able, she collected fourteen of them, including Ninepence, Francis, and Boa Boa. Together they made a new home in the back room of an empty factory. The older girls took in sewing projects, called piecework because they were paid a tiny amount for each piece they sewed. The older boys found odd jobs, such as carrying loads for people or gardening. When they pooled all their money, they had just enough to buy food each day.

Gradually, as Gladys became stronger and able to think more clearly, she went back to missionary work. Ninepence was old enough to take care of the family while Gladys was away.

On one of her mission trips, Gladys took a long trek into Tibet with a Chinese Christian doctor. While there, they were invited to spend a week in a lamasery. As she and the doctor climbed up the steep mountain to the lamasery, Gladys had the feeling the monks inside had been waiting for them. When they arrived, she found that indeed they had been. The head lama himself proudly showed her a gospel tract, which had been glued to the wall. It read, "For God so loved the world that he gave his only begotten Son (John 3:16)." The head lama told Gladys how they had been waiting for three years for someone to come who could tell them more about this God. When they'd heard Gladys and her companion singing Christian hymns in the valley below, they knew they were the ones who could explain the verse to them.

Night after night, the five hundred Lamaist monks listened to Gladys and the doctor preach. Many monks asked Gladys to pray with them or asked questions about the Christian faith. Several years later, Gladys learned that the Communists had destroyed the lamasery, as they had destroyed many other churches and temples in an attempt to remove all outward signs of religion in China. But Gladys knew that among the monks there were those who had truly believed the gospel message and that the Communists could never destroy them.

Wherever Gladys went she shared the gospel message. She worked for a time in a leper colony, where she urged all the newly converted lepers to pray for the local prison. Gladys began preaching in the prison day after day until many of the prisoners became Christian converts. Everywhere she went, it seemed, Chinese people were searching for the true God to help and guide them.

Even though they had already been through so much war and hardship, many Chinese people sensed that the worst was still to come. And it was. Once the war with Japan was over, Gladys witnessed even more bloodshed and brutality. The cruelest thing of all was that this time it was not an outside country inflicting the damage. The Chinese themselves were destroying each other. The tremendous disruption the war with Japan had brought to China had created an opportunity for the Communist party to grab more political control. Now the Communists were in a bitter fight with Nationalist Chinese forces for control of the country. In the north, the Communists seemed to be winning the fight, but at a terrible cost to the Chinese people.

As the fighting raged on, Gladys was asked by the Methodist church to become an evangelist for them. Refugees were still flooding into the area from all over China, and the Methodist church, like all Christian churches in China, had too few trained workers to help. Most foreign missionaries either had been sent home or were still held in concentration camps. Gladys agreed to do it, but only on the condition that she could continue her other work as well. Once more, Gladys was working long hours with little sleep and little food, but she was doing what she loved. When she preached, hundreds of people listened to her, and many became Christian converts. They were from all walks of life. Some were poor refugees who owned nothing but the tattered clothes they wore. Others were people who still held high positions in Chinese society. A large number of students at the local university also became converts, and Gladys encouraged them in their new faith.

Within months, the Communist party took control of the university. It made each of its five hundred students fill out a long questionnaire. Some of the questions were very strange, some even funny, like *How many children does your uncle have? How much money did your grandfather have when he died?* But the last question had dangerous implications for Christians. *What political party do you support? If you are for the government (Communists) put a circle. If you are against it put an "X."*

For each student, answering this question was a serious matter. To draw a circle was to say you were for the new government, which meant you and your family would be favored with good jobs and good money. To put an "X" meant that you were against the government and you would be marked for life and not be allowed good jobs or opportunities in your own country. Each student carefully considered his or her answer. When the circles and X's were counted, the officials were furious. Two hundred questionnaires had X's on them. The government had to find out what was happening. It was not difficult to discover. Student after student told about their conversion to Christianity through Gladys's preaching and explained that they now supported Jesus Christ and no one else.

Of course, this made the leaders of the Communist party very angry. They needed every student's loyalty, and so the three hundred students who had drawn circles on the questionnaire were called to a secret meeting. They were told to harass the Christian students any way they could until the Christian students agreed to support the Communists. A month later, the questionnaire was given again. This time when the papers were collected, there were even more X's than before. Instead of the Communists changing the Christian students' minds, it had worked the other way around!

Again, the circle drawers were called together. They were told by the Communists they must do more to stop the Christians. So prayer meetings were broken up, and Christian students were beaten in darkened alleys. But at the end of a month, not one of the Christian students was ready to support the Communists. In fact, they were more determined than ever not to support them. This angered the Communists very much. They assigned ten Communist supporters to each Christian student to break them down. The Christian students were not allowed to talk to each other, and they were constantly mocked by their companions. Every movement they made and every word they said was recorded. After three months of this, the Communist party called an open meeting in the town square. Gladys was there, praying for the students.

Over two hundred students were marched into the square, heavily guarded by Communist troops. A man clutching a sheath of papers climbed onto a box. He picked up the first sheet of paper and read a name loudly. A seventeen-year-old girl stepped forward from the group of prisoners. Gladys recognized her as a member of a family from Peking that before the war had been very wealthy. The girl was one of the newest converts. Gladys shivered as she thought about the pressure the girl had been living under for the previous three months.

The Communist official cleared his throat. He looked directly at the girl. "Who do you support now?" he asked.

The crowd was hushed. The girl spoke loudly and clearly. "Sir, three months ago, I thought Jesus Christ was real, and I thought the Bible was true. Now after three months of your hatred, I *know* Jesus Christ is real, and I *know* the Bible is true."

The official, his face turned white with rage, yelled to one of the soldiers on his left. The teenage girl was pulled roughly into the center of the square and shoved to her knees. With one swift movement the Communist soldier drew his sword and sliced the girl's head off. Gladys buried her own head in her hands. All she could do was pray the same prayer Mrs. Lawson had taught her, the one she had prayed after seeing her name on the wanted poster in Yangcheng. "If they must die, let them not be afraid of death, but let there be a meaning, O God, in their dying."

As much as she wanted to flee from the terrible sight, Gladys stayed while each of the more than two hundred students was asked whether he or she would support the Communist government. Even though they knew for certain they were only moments from death, not one of them said they supported the Communists. Every one of them was beheaded.

As Gladys walked slowly home after the brutality in the town square, she wept bitterly for what China was becoming.

Gradually, over the next year, it became more difficult for Gladys to continue her missionary work. She was being watched most of the time, and while she didn't fear death or imprisonment for herself, she was concerned that she was drawing attention to many other local Christians and putting their lives in danger.

After much prayer, Gladys decided to move to Shanghai, where she was introduced to a group of influential Chinese Christians who told her about a local society they had formed at the end of the war. The society had collected money from around the world and now used it to send German missionaries and orphaned missionary children back to Germany. German missionaries had been put in a difficult position during the Second World War, which had ended a year before. Their financial support from Germany had been cut off, and countries at war with Germany would not help them. Many German missionaries had died of starvation in China as a result, and those who had lived through the war were weak and in need of medical treatment.

Gladys met the leaders of the society and learned from them that they had located everyone they thought they could help, everyone who was German, that is. As the leaders talked to Gladys, they became convinced that the last few hundred dollars in their fund should be used to send her back to England. Even though it had been seven years since the trek with the children from Yangcheng to Fufeng, Gladys had never fully recovered. She needed more medical help and lots of rest, but since she had no money for a trip back to England for this, the society agreed to pay for the trip.

At first, Gladys did not want to go back to England. China was now her home, and Gladys intended to live and die on Chinese soil. Eventually, however, she accepted the ticket as God's way of telling her it was time to return to England.

Two months later, after traveling by ship from Shanghai and then by train, Gladys once again stood on the platform of Liverpool Street Railway Station in London. It was hard for her to believe she was standing where it had all begun seventeen years before when she boarded the train for Tientsin in China. She had experienced the adventure of a lifetime.

Gladys waited as the passengers from the train disappeared down the platform. When they were gone, only she, dressed in a long Chinese dress, her graying hair pulled firmly back into a bun, and an elderly couple were left standing on the platform. Gladys thought the elderly couple looked disappointed, as though the person they'd come to meet hadn't been on the train. As the couple turned to leave, the elderly woman looked more closely at Gladys and frowned. Then the couple rushed towards her. It was her parents. They had all changed so much over their seventeen years apart that they hadn't recognized each other at first. With tears streaming down their cheeks, they hugged each other.

Gladys and her mother walked along the platform arm in arm. Anyone watching might have thought the two women were sisters, with Gladys being the older, more frail of the two.

It was many months before Gladys felt comfortable in England again. She often forgot where she was and spoke in Mandarin Chinese instead of English, and always there was an ache in her heart for the people in China. Sometimes she would get headaches and feel disoriented, the result of the blow to her head with the rifle butt in Tsechow. She received some medical treatment for the condition, but it continued to be a problem for the rest of her life.

One thing Gladys hadn't counted on when she returned to England was being famous. She had no idea that during the time she'd been in China, her mother had been giving talks on "Our Gladys in China." Also, many people had read the *Time* magazine article. Gladys was a little embarrassed that so many people knew about her, but this fame was nothing compared to what was to come.

Reporters from the big London newspapers came to interview her, and the BBC included her in a radio series it was producing on war heroes. This led to a radio play about her, which led to a book being written about her life in and around Yangcheng. From there, a Hollywood movie was made starring Ingrid Bergman as Gladys. It was an instant hit, and Gladys Aylward became a household name. Her amazing adventures in China became much more widely known than those of explorer Sir Francis Younghusband, who had employed her as a housemaid many years before.

Whenever she could, Gladys used her fame to help Chinese people. She toured the British Isles and Europe, asking Christians to pray for China. She dined with heads of state and met Queen Elizabeth. She set up collection points for warm clothing, which was shipped to the island of Formosa (Taiwan), where many Chinese people had fled after the Communists took control of the main-land of China. Gladys also worked with the hun-dreds of Chinese refugees streaming into Liverpool and other port cities in England. She helped them to learn English and invited them to church services in their own language. She wrote constantly to her children and the orphans she'd led across the mountains. Ninepence was married with a son and still lived on the mainland, though many of the oth-ers had made their way to Formosa.

All of this was not enough for Gladys, however. She wanted to go "home." She wanted to be back among the people and culture she loved. After ten years in England, she decided it was time to return to her people. However, she couldn't reenter main-land China. No foreigners could at that time, whether they had Chinese citizenship before the Communists took over or not. Instead, in early 1957, Gladys left England by ship, headed for Formosa, where she could freely live and work among the Chinese people.

Once again, Gladys Aylward was Ai-weh-deh, the virtuous one. She taught Bible studies, looked after babies and children, and traveled, sharing the gospel message wherever she went. Gladys never stopped working, but, as Mrs. Lawson had been many years before, she was grateful when a young missionary arrived from England to help her.

On New Year's Day, 1970, when she was sixty-seven years old, Gladys went to sleep and never woke up. Her heart had simply stopped beating.

Beside her bed, sleeping peacefully in a crib, was a newborn baby who had been abandoned and brought to Ai-weh-deh to be looked after. Of course, the baby had immediately found a place in Gladys's bedroom and in her heart.

Memorial services were held all over the world for Ai-weh-deh, and more than a thousand people attended her burial service in Taipei, the capital of Taiwan (Formosa). Gladys Aylward's earthly body was buried on a hilltop at Christ's College in Taipei. Her tomb faced the Chinese mainland, where forty adventure-filled years earlier, a young woman had ridden a mule train up the steep trail to Yangcheng, arriving with little more than a Bible and an old, sleeveless fur coat.

Aylward, Gladys. *Gladys Aylward, The Little Woman.* Moody Press, 1970.

Burgess, Alan. *The Small Woman.* E. P. Dutton & Co., 1957.

Swift, Catherine. *Gladys Aylward.* Bethany House Publishers, 1984.

About the Authors

Janet and Geoff Benge are a husband and wife writing team with twenty years of writing experience. Janet is a former elementary school teacher. Geoff holds a degree in history. Originally from New Zealand, the Benges spent ten years serving with Youth With A Mission. They have two daughters, Laura and Shannon, and an adopted son, Lito. They make their home in the Orlando, Florida, area.

Also from Janet and Geoff Benge...

More adventure-filled biographies for ages 10 to 100!

Christian Heroes: Then & Now

Gladys Aylward: The Adventure of a Lifetime • 1-57658-019-9
Nate Saint: On a Wing and a Prayer • 1-57658-017-2
Hudson Taylor: Deep in the Heart of China • 1-57658-016-4
Amy Carmichael: Rescuer of Precious Gems • 1-57658-018-0
Eric Liddell: Something Greater Than Gold • 1-57658-137-3
Corrie ten Boom: Keeper of the Angels' Den • 1-57658-136-5
William Carey: Obliged to Go • 1-57658-147-0
George Müller: The Guardian of Bristol's Orphans • 1-57658-145-4
Jim Elliot: One Great Purpose • 1-57658-146-2
Mary Slessor: Forward into Calabar • 1-57658-148-9
David Livingstone: Africa's Trailblazer • 1-57658-153-5
Betty Greene: Wings to Serve • 1-57658-152-7
Adoniram Judson: Bound for Burma • 1-57658-161-6
Cameron Townsend: Good News in Every Language • 1-57658-164-0
Jonathan Goforth: An Open Door in China • 1-57658-174-8
Lottie Moon: Giving Her All for China • 1-57658-188-8
John Williams: Messenger of Peace • 1-57658-256-6
William Booth: Soup, Soap, and Salvation • 1-57658-258-2
Rowland Bingham: Into Africa's Interior • 1-57658-282-5
Ida Scudder: Healing Bodies, Touching Hearts • 1-57658-285-X
Wilfred Grenfell: Fisher of Men • 1-57658-292-2
Lillian Trasher: The Greatest Wonder in Egypt • 1-57658-305-8
Loren Cunningham: Into All the World • 1-57658-199-3
Florence Young: Mission Accomplished • 1-57658-313-9
Sundar Singh: Footprints Over the Mountains • 1-57658-318-X
C.T. Studd: No Retreat • 1-57658-288-4

Available from YWAM Publishing
1-800-922-2143 / www.ywampublishing.com

Also from Janet and Geoff Benge...
Another exciting biography series!

Heroes of History

Also available:

Unit Study Curriculum Guides
Turn a great reading experience into an even greater
learning opportunity with a Unit Study Curriculum Guide.
Available for select Christian Heroes: Then & Now
and Heroes of History biographies.

Heroes for Young Readers
Written by Renee Taft Meloche • Illustrated by Bryan Pollard

Introduce younger children to the lives of these heroes
with rhyming text and captivating color illustrations!

**All of these series are available from YWAM Publishing
1-800-922-2143 / www.ywampublishing.com**